The Magickal Talismans of K
By Baal Kadmon

Copyright information

Copyright © 2016 by Baal Kadmon

All rights reserved. No part of this book may be reproduced by any mechanical, photographic, or electrical process, or in the form of a recording. Nor may it be stored in a storage/retrieval system nor transmitted or otherwise be copied for private or public use-other than "fair use" as quotations in articles or reviews—without the prior written consent of the Author.

The Information in this book is solely for educational purposes and not for the treatment, diagnosis or prescription of any diseases. This text is not meant to provide financial or health advice of any sort. The Author and the publisher are in no way liable for any use or misuse of the material. No Guarantee of results are being made in this text.

Kadmon, Baal

The Magickal Talismans of King Solomon

–1st ed

Printed in the United States of America

#83761394

Halloween still life with candles and magic objects © samiramayBook Cover Design: Baal Kadmon

At the best of our ability we have credited those who created the pictures based on the research we have conducted. If there are images in the book that have not been given due copyright notice please contact us at resheph@baalkadmon and we will remedy the situation by giving proper copyright credit or we will remove the image/s at your request.

http://www.BAALKADMON.COM

https://www.facebook.com/baal.kadmon

Dedication

I dedicate this book to all of you, my readers and my friends. I also dedicate this book to my patron Saint Expedite.

Disclaimer

Disclaimer: By law, I need to add this statement.

This volume of "Mantra Magick" is for educational purposes only and does not claim to prevent or cure any disease. The advice and methods in this book should not be construed as financial, medical or psychological treatment. Please seek advice from a professional if you have serious financial, medical or psychological issues.

By purchasing, reading and or listening to this book, you understand that results are not guaranteed. In light of this, you understand that in the event that this book or audio does not work or causes harm in any area of your life; you agree that you do not hold Baal Kadmon, Amazon, its employees or affiliates liable for any damages you may experience or incur.

The Text and or audio in this series is copyrighted 2016.

Introduction

Hello and welcome,

Throughout my many years in the occult, I recall many wonderful things. I was enamored by so many different systems that I just had to try them all. For the most part, I did. Some with great success and some not so much. One aspect of the magickal practices that really interested me was the use of talismanic or seal magick. I used all kinds of talisman, and each had its own energy and feel. However, I found the Seals of Solomon (also known as the Talismans of Solomon or the Pentacles of Solomon) to be very interesting. Partly because there is so much information about them, finding the information was a breeze. Well, as easy as it could be in the early 80s. Now one can find almost everything about them on-line. There is one problem though, the information on-line and in many books on the subject are very difficult to understand, and as you may have guessed, if you have read my other books, I don't use conventional methods when I preform magick. I found the convoluted and difficult ways described in the books to be a distraction. A distraction that will most likely turn many people off. It is for this reason I am writing this book.

The idea of writing a book about the seals of Solomon has been on my mind for quite some time, but it was only after my friend, the powerful spell caster and Spiritual/Reiki Healer Wanda at **http://www.thequantummagickshop.com/** emailed me and asked me a few questions about them. We emailed a bit, and she showed me that there is a great need for an easy to understand guide on the Seals of Solomon. It was her inquiry and urging that I decided it was the right time to release a book on the Talismans of Solomon that would be easily understood but also inform on the various Solomonic traditions that are out there. We tend to hyper-focus on the Judeo-Christian aspects

only and for the most part that is what I will also do in this book as well. However, there is also another, just as ancient tradition of Solomonic magick in Muslim tradition as well. I will attempt to synthesize all the information in such a way that will make the use of Solomonic talisman effective and approachable...
With that, let us begin.

King Solomon

I suppose a book about the Talisman of Solomon would not be complete without a chapter about Solomon, the king himself. We tend to think of King David as being the most notable king in the Old Testament. After all, he is referenced much more when it comes to Jewish identity. In many ways, David was more of a brute figure, a fighter and was put on the map with his whole battle with Goliath. His son King Solomon has a much more robust reputation for good or for ill; Solomon achieved much more and was worldlier. His exploits are renowned and makes his father, King David look like a School Marme in many respects. King Solomon is also the focus of many different traditions, not only Judaism, but Islam, Ethiopic Christianity and a few others. In Ethiopic Christianity, Solomon is one of the most important characters second only to Solomon's son Menelik (Not many people know that). In this chapter I will go into this history of Solomon, and then we will continue to other pertinent topics before jumping into the magick.

King Solomon in the Biblical tradition:

Historians generally place King Solomon's reign from 970-931 BC. Although we will be using these same dates, I would like to point out that since there is almost no archeological evidence for the King, the dating is really only a guesstimate.

As I mentioned, he is the son of King David and also the third king of the united Israel. I say united because Israel was not always a United Kingdom. Now when we think of Israel, we see a Jewish nation in which cities such as Tel Aviv and Jerusalem as being under one government. However, in ancient times this was not always the case. The Northern Kingdom of Israel and the southern Kingdom of Judah were at odds. It was under King David that they united but after King Solomon's death, the two divided once again. Since Solomon's blood line is from Judah, it is for this reason Judah is supposedly where the future messiah is to come from. "From The Blood Line of David" as they say.

When His father David died, he took the reins of Israel. He hit the ground running as it were. He dispensed with the people in his father's cabinet and appointed his friends to take on the most important posts of the kingdom, from the religious jobs to the military ones. King Solomon was a bit hawkish and put much of his resources at hand to expanding the military might of his Kingdom. This military might allow him to create military posts and colonies throughout the region. Like his father, he was very good at keeping diplomatic ties; he realized it was often better to approach an enemy with Honey rather than with vinegar. He was a sucker for luxury and thus became known as the richest of all kings. He continued and expanded the trade of luxuries with the Kingdom of Phoenicia to keep the supply coming. I would say he was even decadent; he is reputed to have had 1000 wives and concubines. Surely, many of these arrangements were to solidify alliances, but that still gives you an idea of the type of lifestyle he lived.

What Solomon is most notated for was his construction of the First temple in Jerusalem during his 4th year of reign. It's around this construction where the magickal lore starts to take shape, but before we get into that, we have a lot of ground to cover.

As I mentioned above, Solomon had 1000 wives and concubines. The number according to the bible is 700 wives and 300 concubines. Most were foreign in nature and were mostly used to solidify alliances as stated earlier. The taking of a wife to solidify an alliance was not unusual. The quantity in this case was exceptional and in my estimation a bit mythical in nature. Even Ramses II who had 160 children with 200 wives almost seems unreal, but that was probably true. In short, Solomon was crazy for the ladies. So much so that it got him into some serious trouble. He adored some of them so much that he would do anything to keep them happy. This involved allowing some of them to import and worship their "foreign gods and goddesses" he even allowed and commissioned a temple to the Goddess Ashtoret. To you and me, that sounds rather good. I would love to build a temple to Ashtoret, but to the Jewish people at the time, this was a HUGE infraction. In Kings 11:4 it is stated that Solomon was highly influenced by some of his wives and started to worship some of these idols. This was not something Yahweh would have approved of. The division of the Israelites after his death was his greatest punishment for this behavior.

I am sure Solomon was a swell looking guy, but I think he was loved for his mind and his wealth. His wisdom is also part of the rich magickal tradition surrounding him. Supposedly, much of this knowledge was gleaned from his occult work with spirits; of course, in the bible itself, it will never confess that he obtained knowledge from demons and devils. We will get into that later.

In the bible, more specifically the book of Kings, we see that Solomon truly wanted wisdom and would pray and offer sacrifices to God for it. It was apparent that this was the only thing he truly wanted. He never prayed for riches, I guess because he already had great wealth. Some of his great wisdom can be found in several books of the bible that are ascribed to him such as Ecclesiastes, Lamentations and Proverbs. Many of the sayings in those books were quite downbeat and made one wonder if he also suffered from melancholy. One can also see his wisdom and his erotic side in the "Songs of Solomon." Rabbis like to say that the Song of Solomon was an allegory of God's relationship to Israel. Well, I don't think so, his reputation gives no indication as such, but then again, who am I to say. These books can all be found in the Old Testament; I highly recommend reading them; you will find many of insights are quite profound. Of course, there are other texts ascribed to him, but we will deal with those separately since they are outside the traditional ideas of Solomon.

According to the bible, Solomon died of natural causes when he was about 80 years old. As God promised, as a punishment, the Kingdom of Israel became divided once again, and they were never united from that moment forward.

The Biblical and Ethiopian Christian Tie-in

I just want to backtrack a little and discuss his relationship with the Queen of Ethiopia, and some would say Queen of Yemen as well. The Queen of Sheba, I feel it is a very interesting history since this relationship informs several traditions outside the conventional scriptural accounts. I did not add it to the last section because I wanted to cover both the biblical and Ethiopic versions of this relationship between the two monarchs at the same time since there is significant overlap.

Queen of Sheba most likely ruled the territory that incorporates Yemen, Ethiopia, Eritrea and Somalia. Oddly enough, for such an impactful relationship the bible leaves out significant details of the relationship. From the biblical account, we know that, as I mentioned, Solomon had great wisdom. This attracted the Queen of Sheba (I told you he was known more for his brain). She heard all these wonderful things and decided that she would pay him a visit. As is customary, when you visit royalty, you bring gifts. Sheba did just that. She brought precious stones, incense and exotic spices. Solomon was so enamored of her that in Kings 10:10 it states that Solomon gave her everything she asked, and she left satisfied. As you can see, and as I mentioned earlier, he aimed to please, even at his own peril. In that account, it was Queen Sheba seeking out Solomon. However, in a rabbinic tradition it is the other way around.

Various signs led Solomon to discover her great land and after discovering these signs, he summoned her at once.

The bible doesn't go into great depth but apparently this was enough to spark several traditions, one of which is the Ethiopian Christian ideas of this union.

In the Ethiopian book the Kebra Nagast or Glory of the Kings (which I might cover in a future title) it goes into greater depth. In this account, the Queen and the King "Had union" and she was found pregnant with a son who was later named Menelik. He was a Jewish king but later his dynasty would become a Christian one. It is for this reason I address it as a Christian conception in contrast to a Jewish one. Menelik, the supposed Son of Solomon received a gift from his father, a Replica of the Ark of the Covenant but something happened, somehow the replica was switched, and the real ark was sent off to Menelik. Unto this day, it is believed to be in Ethiopia, and it is currently being guarded by a single priest who will guard it for the rest of days.

As you can imagine, this idea that the original ark is in Ethiopia has only served to heightened Ethiopian prestige of its monarchy. Unfortunately, for us, we can't view the ark and see if it is, in fact, there. Perhaps one day we will.

Before we close this section of the chapter I would like to mention something you might find interesting. In Jewish classical texts, it is also written that Sheba may have had a child with Solomon. The text did not describe this as a good thing. In fact, the texts say that he was punished for this. They contend that the child was the early ancestor of the Babylonian King Nebuchadnezzar II who, some 300 years later destroyed the temple. Their proof is somewhat interesting, suspect and certainly obscure. It is also not directly apparent if you don't know Hebrew. Let me explain.

The name Nebuchadnezzar means, in Akkadian, "Nebu Preserve my first born"; Nebu being the god of knowledge. In Akkadian, like most names of the time, adding a deity to the name was very common; Egyptians did it all the time. I.e. Amenhotep "Amen is pleased" etc. The Rabbis, however, had another interesting take on his name. They use the Hebrew lettering and divided it into three parts. I will transliterate.

נְבוּכַדְנֶצַּר

NEBU - נְבוּ

CHAD - כַדְ

NEZZAR - נֶצַּר

The three sections are as such:

NEBU: is very close to the word "Nevooa" or "prophecy."

CHAD: is the Hebrew word meaning "vessel" or "vase."

NEZZAR: which in the Hebrew is "offspring or descendant"

So they reasoned that Nebu chad nezzar was the descendant of Solomon's child with Sheba that was prophesied to destroy Solomon's temple as a punishment. He contained the seed of that prophecy so to speak. I know it is a long shot, but it was an idea that was floating out there, and some teachers still like to use this clever device. In Judaism, you will find many instances of these kinds of things. I will admit that some are quite compelling and, in my estimation, true and should be considered seriously. This one I am not sure should be heeded, but it is very interesting nonetheless and I won't completely discount it off hand.

Alright, pardon me for that little excursion; let's get back to some history. Let us now examine Islam's ideas of Solomon.

Solomon in Islam:

Solomon is quite prominent in Islamic holy texts. In Quran, alone Solomon is mentioned about 17-18 times. Few people can boast that in the Quran. Like the other traditions about Solomon, he is accepted to be the son of King David and was the King over Israel.

There is however, a critical difference. Despite Solomon's reputation as having control over spirits in the Islamic traditions, he was not punished nor condemned for ever having performed any acts of idolatry like he did in the bible. I.e. temples to Ashterot. That part is completely absent. Not only is it absent, Solomon was considered resilient to idolatry and everything that came with it; it was the children of Israel who backslide into magic and witchcraft, not Solomon. In Quran 2: 102 it states

"And they followed [Israel] what the devils had recited during the reign of Solomon. It was not Solomon, who disbelieved, but the devils disbelieved, teaching people magic and that which was revealed to the two angels at Babylon, Harut and Marut. However, the two angels do not teach anyone, unless they say, "We are a trial, so do not disbelieve by practicing magic." And yet they learn from them that by which they cause separation between a man and his wife. But they do not harm anyone through it except by permission of Allah. And the people learn what harms them and does not benefit them. But the Children of Israel certainly knew that whoever purchased the magic would not have in the hereafter any share. And wretched is that for which they sold themselves, if they only knew."

This seems contradictory to the Islamic tradition about Solomon that we will see in a moment. The Quran, we will discover later described Solomon as controlling the Jinn. If that is not magic and witchcraft, I am not sure what is? You will see what I mean. In Quran 27:15-17, Quran 21:79-82, Quran 27:16 and Quran 38: 35-38 all describe how wise Solomon was and how much power he had. The verses go on to say that he had the ability to communicate with birds, control the weather. AND as I intimated earlier, it says that God granted him magickal and supernatural powers over Jinn and demons upon request. Did Solomon perform a ritual to gain these powers? We can't know, although other texts suggest that he did.

The manner of death in Islam suggests that he died of natural causes as the bible also suggests, however, something odd happens during Solomon's death in the Islamic conception. Quran 34:14 When Solomon died, he was in a standing position praying and holding his cane. The cane apparently propped him up so he did not fall. He remained in a standing position, and everyone, including the spirits still thought that he was alive. Oddly enough, God sends a termite to slowly eat Solomon's cane; with time, the cane weakens and Solomon falls. It was only then that everyone learned that he was dead. The moral of the story apparently is to prove that people and spirits don't know anything but only God knows the truth. Interesting right?

There you have it. I did not want to go very deep into his history since that is not the goal of this book, but at least you have some idea of the type of man he was perceived to be. In the next few chapters, we will discuss talismanic magick some of the magickal traditions surrounding Solomon and then, we will move on to the talismans themselves and the magick. I know it's a lot, but this background information is in my opinion, vital and, well, it makes for some interesting conversations with your friends and family.

A Brief History of the Talisman in Jewish Tradition

Talismanic magick and the usage of Seals in general are as old as humanity itself. Often, Talismans and Amulets are confused, although there is significant overlap. Amulets are generally used for protection whereas talismans are used for good luck and to bring about certain outcomes such as to attract love, money, etc. Although I will use talisman and amulets interchangeably in this text, I just wanted to get that out of the way that technically, they are different.

Talismans are taken very seriously and have various classes based on HOW they are used.

The most common category of Talismans is those that are worn on the body for protection.

The Second common category of Talismans are the ones that are hung over a bed to heal sickness or to ward off demons.

The Third Most common category of Talisman is used for medicinal purposes of various kinds. They can either be immersed in water to "charge" the water with healing energies that are emanating from this talisman or worn on the person. An additional way this is used is by inscribing the letters from a talisman on food, so the person could eat, and the healing energies will transfer into the body.

The fourth way to use talismans is for various other reasons such as to conquer one's enemies, to gain wealth, to find love, acquire knowledge and attain magickal powers, etc.

Fifth Category of talisman is the bible itself. The bible is often used as a standalone talisman. It is either placed on the chest of the individual or under the pillow or bed.

The Jewish tradition alone is very well-known for its talismanic magick and we will mostly focus on it because that is technically the tradition in which the Solomonic Talismans emerge. Solomonic magick in general, however, is broader as you will see in a future chapter.

Unto this day many Jewish people, especially those who come from Middle Eastern countries tend to have greater affinity with Talismans. Often in this tradition, it is called "Camea" Or "Kamea." The Solomonic seals are in this class. Generally speaking, the Talismans tend to be comprised of angelic names, names of God, as well as scriptural passages from the Old Testament. Seldom will you find images since the bible has several clear Anti-Idolatry and graven image clauses, although you might see that one or two have crept in. You will see what I mean later.

A famous Judaic amulet is the one against "Lilith" The demoness and first wife of Adam, who is considered the cause of Sudden Infant Death Syndrome and Night Paralysis/Night terrors; she is also the prototype for the Succubus. This seal is found in a Jewish magickal text called " Sefer Raziel Hamalach" Or the Book of Raziel the Angel. Please see image.

Amulet against Lilith in Sefer Raziel Hamalach

All Religious Jews use talismans every day and may not even consider it as such. The Tallit which is the prayer shawl they wear in the synagogue is a Talisman as is the tiztzit which is the fringed corners that is worn daily. It serves as a remembrance of God and his special connection to them. The same applies to the Mezuzah which is nailed to the door posts of most Jewish homes; this too would qualify as a talisman since it is a parchment paper with biblical inscriptions, which is then rolled up and placed in a holder. And of course, the most famous Jewish amulet is the Star of David.

As an interesting side story, one of the greatest and most controversial incidences in German Jewish history was caused by a talisman. A Man by the name of Jonathan Eybeschuetz, who was the rabbi of Hamburg Germany, was accused by another German Rabbi named Jacob Emden of having created a Talisman with the name of Shabbetai Zevi. Shabbetai Zevi was a man who proclaimed himself the messiah in 1668. Turns out, of course, that he was a false messiah. Despite that he was highly influential. Shabbetai has been roundly denounced as a heretic throughout the Jewish world. To be accused of supporting anything related to Shabbetai Zevi was and still is considered a huge heresy.

(If you would like to know more about Shabbetai Zevi , please refer to the additional resources chapter for books that I recommend on him as well as on other related topics. This additional resource chapter will also serve as a bibliography for the historical sources in this book.)

Suffice it to say, most of the Abrahamic religions from antiquity through the Middle Ages used and believed in the power of Talisman.

On the outset, it would seem rather anti-Christian to believe in such things, but it was allowed when it was the bible or a crucifix and if you were Catholic, medals dedicated to Saints would and are still allowed as Amulets and talisman. I am not Catholic, but I for one have a St Expedite Medal.

In Islam, Talismans were used as well, but it was viewed as a superstition and in some places, it is forbidden. It was said that Allah hated 10 things, and talismans were among them. However, as with every tradition, people have always found a need to use magick. As I have said in my other books... Magick is in our blood.

Solomon the Magician in Islam and Judaism

As you read in a previous chapter, Solomon was quite a guy, we saw that he was a hit with the ladies and as the books say it was for his "brain." He had unlimited wealth and has the ability to control nature and spirits. In this chapter, we will discuss the origins of Solomon's reputation for using magick and spirits. You will see that it is quite robust in some traditions and not as much in others. We will start with the Islamic conception first since its more transparent. What I mean by this is that Solomon is mentioned to have direct power over demons and Jinn IN THE QURAN. That would be tantamount to the Disciples calling Jesus a Magician in the Canonical Gospels. In other traditions, Solomon's connection to magick is written in apocryphal books and exegetical books on the bible but not in the bible itself. Quran sort of breaks the mold but with a slight twist. Let's take a very quick look.

(Some of this Section is an excerpt from my book "Jinn Magick")

It is said that King Solomon had great powers over the Jinn and angels for that matter, but it also known that Solomon gained his vast wisdom by calling upon these forces. This was a rich ancient tradition that went even further back than Jesus and lives quite vibrantly in Islam. The reason we know this is because Jesus makes an interesting if not somewhat veiled reference to Solomon's power. Matthew 12:42" The queen of Sheba will also stand up against this generation on judgment day and condemn it, for she came from a distant land to hear the Wisdom of Solomon. Now someone greater than Solomon is here--but you refuse to listen."

Although Jesus is mentioning that he is of greater wisdom than Solomon, he still mentioned Solomon because he knows that

Solomon was considered the wisest person on earth. This, of course, can be gleaned from reading the Old Testament book of kings, as well as the Jewish literature books Ecclesiastes, Lamentations and Proverbs that are often ascribed to Solomon as I said earlier. There is however, another passage that is a bit more direct in the book of "The Testament of Solomon," which is an Old Testament pseudepigraphical book which is littered with direct references that Solomon used demons to build the temple we spoke about earlier. He also used the demons for other purposes. Although in those books they often refer to them as demons, in Islam, they call them Jinn, which are not exactly demons. I explain that in "Jinn Magick." The Testament of Solomon is in the public domain and can be readily found online by searching the title. It is the above-mentioned book that the greater keys of Solomon and other magickal texts were ultimately derived. There is another text that references Solomon's use of Jinn and demons; it is called "The Apocalypse of Adam." This is a Gnostic Gospel that was found in the Cache of Gnostic gospels at Nad Hammadi. This Gospel contains references to a legend in which Solomon sends out his spiritual minions to seek a virgin who ran away from him. This text may perhaps be the earliest mentioning that Solomon controlled spirits and made them his servants and slaves. The above leads me to believe that even Jesus knew of the fact that Solomon has this kind of control over demons and angels. And by saying, "...a greater one than Solomon is here..." he was stating that he too has this power. We actually know that he did. Jesus is found controlling demons as many as 25 referenced to him "casting" them out. He clearly had this power as well.

But I digress, Solomon not only controlled these entities, they actually were ever present and around him all the time, they were also part of his army. The Jinn or demons as we understand them to be in the west have always remained in the service of Solomon. It is understood that he kept them in bondage, and that they weren't with him out of their own free will. The Quran states:

" And before Solomon were marshalled his hosts, of jinn and men and birds, and they were all kept in order and ranks". (Quran 27:17).

In Islam in general, there is a rich tradition based on these spirits that he controlled. Solomon and his powers were also referenced in the 1001 Arabian nights. In one of the more popular stories from this collection recounts that a "Genie" or Jinn had made King Solomon angry and was banished to be locked up in a bottle and thrown into the Sea. (The Arabian night is where the Genie in the bottle story comes from, by the way).

So this poor genie is locked in the bottle which was sealed with Solomon's seal. It was said he was freed many hundreds of years late when he was found by a fisherman. Several other stories within Islam describe Solomon's connection to Demons and magick.

The Muslim Scholar Ibn al-Nadmin in his book Kitab al-Fihrist described quite a bit about the Jinn and what days of the week belong to them and their various kingdoms. It was found that many of the names of the Jinn are in fact, the same demons mentioned in the Testament of Solomon, I mentioned earlier.

With that, let us move on to the Jewish Solomonic Magickal references.

Solomonic References in Jewish Rabbinic Literature:

There is quite a bit about Solomon's magickal life in Jewish texts but not directly in the biblical texts like in the Quran. As I mentioned earlier, Solomon only prayed for Wisdom in the bible but the rabbis said this praying also bestowed upon him great powers. They even went on to say his 1000 wives were due to this magickal power of magnetism. The rabbis say that the demons and spirits he controlled brought him exotic plants, precious stones and the like. He was able to harness this power through a magickal ring which is known as the Seal of Solomon, which is most likely the same seal referred to in the 1001 Arabian nights.

(As an interesting side note, The Seal of Solomon, in some of the extant legends was also known as the Ring of Aandaleeb, and was much sought after as a symbol of power. In many legends, different groups or individuals attempted to obtain it, by hook or by crook).

As I mentioned, Solomon was known to have used these spirits to help build the first temple of Israel.

The temple according to rabbinic legends was entirely created by these beings that he magickally compelled. The large multi-ton stones needed to build the temple would rise and would be put in place by these invisible helpers. A very interesting aspect of this story that I read long ago is that although the spirits lifted and placed the stones, the stones were cut by something called a "Shamir" which according to the Midrash Tehillim (an exegetical text) the Shamir was a kind of worm that would, by simply touching stone could make it break asunder or cut the stone perfectly as desired. The text says that this "worm" was brought to Solomon by an eagle who found it in "Paradise." Paradise in the Jewish tradition always refers to the "Garden of Eden" Do you think Adam and Eve encountered this worm?

Some other rabbis think it came from the demonic worlds. In either case, isn't that a weird story? A Magickal Stone cutting worm is probably one of the weirder things I have heard of. I can see how such a worm could come in handy though. Makes me wonder, did this same worm help the Egyptians or the Mayans cut their nearly perfect stone monuments? Inquiring Minds want to know. I guess it's as good an answer as any other that has been posited to date. ?

Alright, we are almost to the magick; we have 2 more chapters until we get to the Talismans. Trust me; this is all information that can only help you gain an understanding of Solomonic magick.

The Testament of King Solomon

In this chapter, we will discuss the Old Testament apocryphal text called "The Testament of King Solomon." The reason I am including this in the book is because this is by far the only "scriptural" book that is almost entirely dedicated to Solomon's magickal powers over spirits. It is also the book that is the very foundation of Geotic magick. In fact, some of the demons in Geotia first appear in the testament of Solomon.

The Testament of King Solomon was originally written in Greek, this testament is a bit complex in that despite it being ascribed to King Solomon himself who was around about 970 B.C. It appears to be a much more recent text, perhaps written around the first-century A.D. Could this be what Jesus was really referring to when he mentions Solomon's power? Perhaps...I guess it depends how early in the 1st century it was written. Some also say it could have been written as late as the 5th century as well. Another thing that seems suspicious is that many elements of the book contain Christian and Greek mythological themes. Despite this, some could say that Solomon did have access to this information. Rabbinic tradition also states that he knew all knowledge, including future knowledge. Oddly enough the Ethiopian Glory of Kings I mentioned earlier states that he had a flying object, like a plane, I guess you could say. Referring to a journey over the Red Sea, it states: "each was raised over the Red Sea traveling like an eagle when his body glideth over the wind." I think all that is unlikely, but I have heard of stranger things. Maybe the Rabbis are right. I will leave that to you, the reader to decide.

The testament, I must admit is not a thrilling read, but it is still interesting nonetheless. Here is a quick synopsis of this testament. It starts pretty quickly with the demons. A Demon by the name of Ornias was harming this young man who was apparently well-liked by King Solomon. He harmed him like most demons would; he stole half his money and slowly, through the young man's thumbs sucked his energy out of him. Solomon hears of this and in his prayer, the archangel Michael appears to him and gives him a ring. The ring of course is this famous " Seal of Solomon" we have heard so much about. Solomon gives the young man this ring that proceeds to throw the ring at the demon who is vexing him. This act places the demon under his control. In an interesting twist, Solomon orders the demon Ornias to imprint the ring on the prince of all demons " Beelzebul." Yes, Beelzebul as opposed to Beelzebub. I am wondering if this was an intentional misspelling or meant to suggest there is another demon with a very similar name. From what I know of demonology, this should be Beelzebub.

Now that the prince of demons is under Solomon's control, he forces Beelzebul to call upon his entire demon race to construct the first temple for him. The testament would be rather dull if it was only about the construction of the temple, but it gets deeper and a bit more interesting. We start to meet certain demons who are responsible for various kinds of things. Since these demons are now under Solomon's control, they were also compelled to give him the information needed to banish them.

In one of the more interesting and slightly baffling demonic encounters, we find Solomon sending one of his boy servants with the ring to capture a wind demon who is causing trouble in the land of Arabia. The boy is given very specific instructions. He must hold a wineskin against the winds and with the ring in front of it, and when the bag is full, he ties it up. Apparently, that was all it took to capture this great wind demon.

This wind demons name is Ephippas and it was through his power that some of the larger cornerstones would be moved around. I guess he would cause a great wind to lift them. It is the encounter with this demon where we find an apparent

Christian theme. While Ephippas was working on the temple it was clear he was not happy. Solomon approaches the demon, and they talk. Turns out the demon wasn't lamenting his plight with Solomon but of the future arrival of one who will be able to defeat all demons. He describes this man as 'a man who will be born of a virgin, who will be betrayed by the Jews and crucified by the Romans.'. I'd say that is a very Christian theme, wouldn't you agree? Now one can say that demons can see the future so could this account be possible in the time of Solomon? I suppose so, but I am not so sure. I have a feeling it was redacted later by Christians who wanted the book to steer more towards their agenda.

Ephippas after saying this to Solomon continues on with his work, he and a demon from the Red Sea brought a beautiful purple column to add to the temple. The name of this Red Sea demon is Ameloith. This demon has some very interesting credentials. He claimed that he was the demon who supported the pharaoh's magicians against Moses. Oddly enough he also confesses to hardening Pharaoh's heart.

In a brazen account that smacks of Greek Mythology is the encounter that Solomon has with the seven demon sisters. Oddly enough they state that they live in Mount Olympus. This is a clear reference to the seven demon sisters who represent the Pleiades in Greek Mythology. Another interesting connection to Greek Mythology is the demon Enepsigos; who tells Solomon that he is associated with the moon and can appear as a woman with 3 heads? HEKATE ANYONE?

Solomon eventually concludes the testament with a warning to all of humanity that we should avoid becoming like him, and that we should be mindful of our actions since we don't always know what they will lead us to in the future. That's pretty sound advice.

There are other odd stories from this testament; I highly recommend that you take a read of it. I will provide my recommendation for the best translation in the Additional resources chapter.

In this chapter, we gave a broad overview that showed that a Solomonic magickal tradition exists, in the next chapter, we will cover another foundational book. This book is, in fact, where the Talismans, we are going to use are derived from. Then after that, we will discuss each Talisman.

The Key of Solomon

We have come to our final chapter regarding the Historical context of the Solomonic magickal tradition. Although the book I am covering in this chapter is where we derive the Talismans, we won't be spending a huge amount of time on it because it is mostly complex and in my opinion, unnecessary rituals that might have seemed good in the context of its day, but is wholly unnecessary today. I might even argue that back in its day it was also a bit too much.

The Key of Solomon aka Clavicula Salomonis in Latin and Mafteach Shelomoh in Hebrew is probably something you are familiar with. The Solomonic talismans or pentacles as sometimes they are referred to as in the book are by far the most popular of the talismans and seals in the occult tradition. In every book on seals and talismans that I have seen, they reference these that are present in this book. As I mentioned in the introduction, they are simply the most easily accessible. In modern times, the one who put it on the Map was the great occultist S. L. MacGregor Mathers in 1889.

Many historians place the writing of this book somewhere between the 15-16 centuries in Italy. There are quite a few versions of this book, some conform almost to the letter, and some seem to be adjusted and appear to have drastic changes done to them. Most agree, however, that the Latin and Italian versions of this book seem most complete. However, there appears to be a Greek version that may have been the inspiration for those versions. The Greek one is called "The Magickal Treatise of Solomon." I happened to take a look at that one, and it is very interesting indeed. There are two versions of this in Hebrew as well. You can find it at the British Museum. Scholars do not believe the Hebrew is the original but a derivative copy of the Latin and Italian versions.

According to the Solomonic legend surrounding this book, it is said that Solomon wrote all this and passed it on to his Son Rehoboam, who was to hide the book upon Solomon's death. Rehoboam did this, and the book was lost to history. That is until Many years later, Babylonian philosophers discovered the book at Solomon's tomb. Some say the Tomb is still in Israel somewhere. So these philosophers would not read the book, so they asked God for help in understanding the text. As they prayed, an angel of God appears to them and miraculously gives them the ability to understand the text. As is the case in most stories of this nature, this ability to read the text did not come free. The philosophers had to take a vow that they would never share the information with anyone who was evil. In order to ensure this, the book itself has a spell cast upon it. If a person obtains the book and is of evil nature, the magick will not work. Well, suffice it to say, the spell didn't work because plenty of people of ill intent and ill repute have since used it with great success.

The book as you may have surmised is a Grimoire of spells and incantations. The book itself is divided into two sections or two books if you will. The rituals that one finds in this book are called "operations and experiments." I will not address them as such since I feel it takes it away from what they really are. Unlike the other books ascribed to Solomon such as those that employ the powers of the 72 demons, the rituals in this book are mostly addressed directly to "God." We will keep to this standard when working with the various talismans in this book.

The text itself is a bit complicated and speaks of rituals so difficult I HIGHLY doubt that anyone has the time our ability to really perform them as prescribed. As you know, for me, it is about simplicity and in this book, I will remain true to that tradition. I will strip the complexity out of this system in such a way that you will find working with the Talismans not only easy but also more effective. Sure, there might be some detail in the seals themselves, but I will parse through those as well so it will be accessible.

As I mentioned, the book is divided into two parts.

Part 1

It contains all prayers, curses, conjurations and invocations that call forth and bind demons and the spirits of the dead. It also has a few spells for love, to find stolen items, etc.

Part 2

It is in this section, we find the talismans. It also contains the elaborate rituals need for purification and the like. It also suggests various animal sacrifices. We won't be dealing with that.

With that said, let us take a look at the seals and their respective meanings. He seals we will look at are the popular renditions that are most accessible. Let us take a look.

The Magickal Talismans of King Solomon

We are finally at the chapter that will describe the Talismans. I will itemize each one and give you as full a description as possible. There are 44 in total. Some contain Hebrew names and Hebrew inscriptions. I will translate them, so you will have a better understanding as to what you are dealing with. Let us Begin.

First Pentacle of Saturn

This Talisman is used to compel others to do your will.

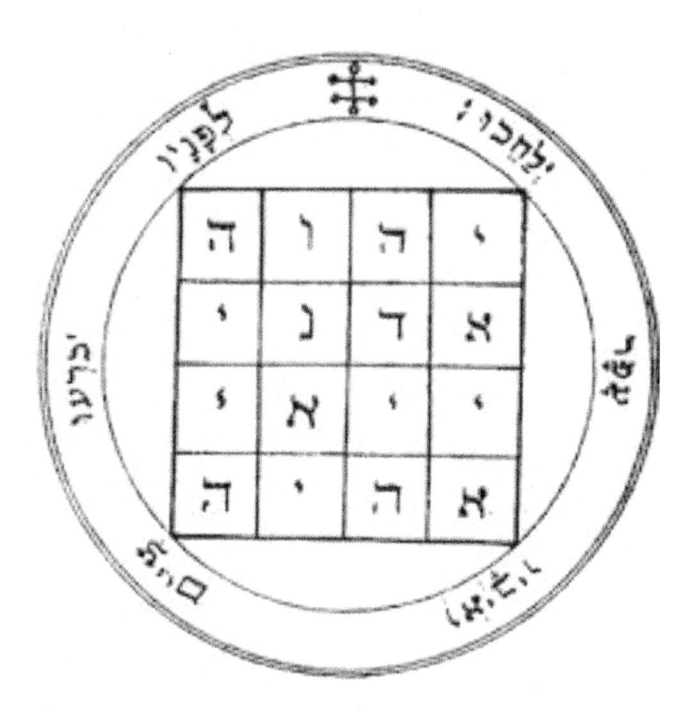

This Talisman is often used to compel people, but it is also used to compel spirits to do your will.

The Hebrew letters in the square are the four, four lettered names of God:–YHVH, Yod, Hey, Vav, Hey; Aleph, Dalet, Noon, Yod-- Adoneye; Yod, Yod, Aleph, Yod,--Yiai and Aleph. Hey, Yod, Hey—Eh-ee-yeh. The Hebrew scripture is from Psalms 72:9: 'May the desert tribes bow before him and his enemies lick the dust.'

Day of week: Saturn

Candle Color: Black

We will discuss how to charge it and use it in the coming chapters.

Second Pentacle of Saturn

If you are in any kind of competition, whether it be sports, person or business, this Talisman works wonders.

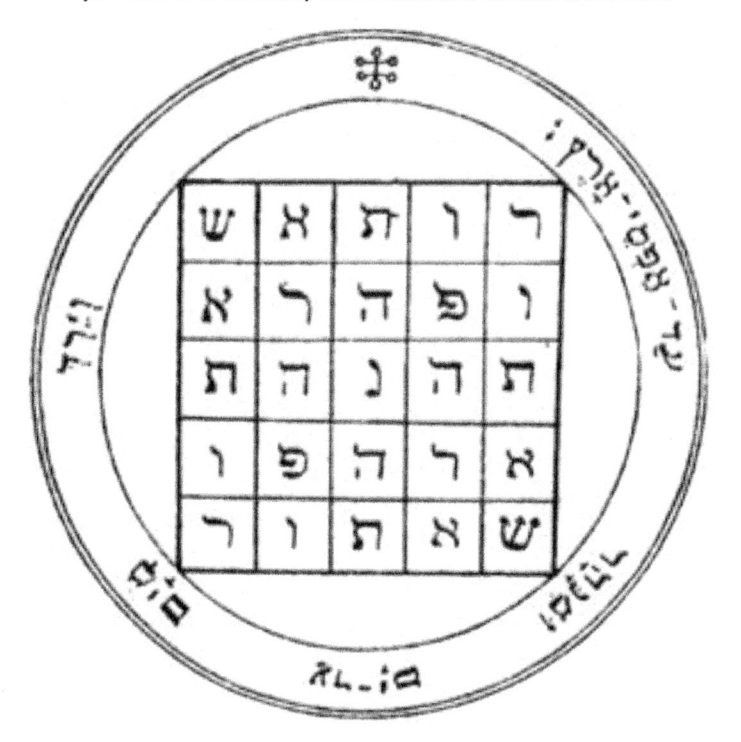

If you have studied seals before you will recognize the very famous "SATOR" square. This square is ancient since they have found he square in a few ancient sites; more specifically first in the Ruins of Pompeii. It is mentioned the most in books on magick from the medieval period. Although there are several traditions on the Square and its function, some believe it has "General" magickal powers and therefore, in this seal it is meant as an enhancer. There are 25 letters in the square; this will become important in a moment.

The Hebrew verse around it is from Psalms 72:8 "May he rule from sea to sea and from the River to the ends of the earth."

In Hebrew, that verse also contains 25 letters.

Day of week: Saturn

Candle Color: Black

We will discuss how to charge it and use it in the coming chapters.

Third Pentacle of Saturn

This is a good seal to carry around to defend yourself from the plots against you hatched by others against you. It is also an excellent talisman to repel evil spirits.

This is a good seal to carry around to defend yourself from the plots against you hatched by others against you. It is also an excellent talisman to repel evil spirits.

From top moving clock wise contains the names of angels who will help you to defend yourself from people or spirits. The angels are:

Omliel: This angel will help bind other spirits that are trying to harm you.

Anachiel: This angel will help you with the people who are trying to harm you. It is also a good angel for those who are shy.

Arauchia: This angel will help you detect and protect you from the lies and betrayals of others.

Anatzchia: it is not clear what his exact purpose it, but he is most probably used as an enhancement to the other angels.

Day of week: Saturn

Candle Color: Black

We will discuss how to charge it and use it in the coming chapters.

Fourth Pentacle of Saturn

To be used in all rituals that deal with death, ruin and destruction. Please be careful with this one

The Hebrew surrounding the triangle is from a very famous passage in the Old Testament and is part of a prayer that is recited every day by Jewish people across the global.

"Hear, O Israel: The LORD our God, the LORD is one." Deuteronomy 6:4. This verse serves as an enhancement to the following verse that is in the outer circle. Psalms 109:18 " He wore cursing as his garment; it entered into his body like water, into his bones like oil."

Day of week: Saturn

Candle Color: Black

We will discuss how to charge it and use it in the coming chapters.

Fifth Pentacle of Saturn

To be used for protection not only in your day to day life but also against evil spirits. It is also used to safeguard your personal belongings.

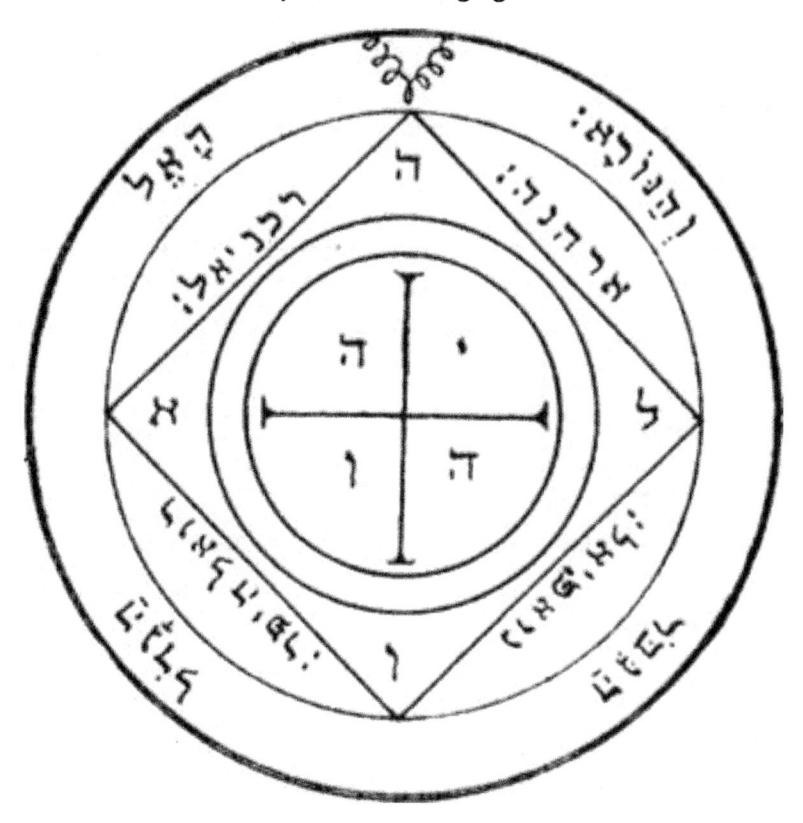

The name within the inner circle is the great four-letter name of God YHVH, Yod, Hey, Vav, Hey. The name within the square from top moving clockwise is Aleph, Lamed, Vav, Aleph, ELOHA.

The Angelic names right outside the triangle are:

Arehanah: Is the angel that will show you how to live a proper life.

Rakhaniel: Is the bestower of wisdom and will power.

Roelhaiphar: The preventer of tragedies and bad things.

Noaphiel: It Appears to be an enhancer to the other angels

The Hebrew inscription written around the circle going counter clockwise is "For the LORD, your God is God of gods and Lord of lords, the great God, mighty and awesome, who shows no partiality and accepts no bribes." Deuteronomy 10.17

Day of week: Saturn

Candle Color: Black

We will discuss how to charge it and use it in the coming chapters.

Sixth Pentacle of Saturn

This seal is also one that should be used with great caution. If you have an enemy, you particularly do not like, this seal can be used to send them ghosts, poltergeist and demons as a means of torment.

The Hebrew words aren't from the bible; it is not clear where they are from, but it says, "Set upon him a wicked one to be ruler over him, and let Satan stand at his right hand."

Day of week: Saturn

Candle Color: Black

We will discuss how to charge it and use it in the coming chapters.

Seventh Pentacle of Saturn

I am not sure why one would need this, but this seal is to cause or worsen an earthquake.

The Hebrew angelic names are of the various orders of angels instead of individual ones.

Chayot Ha Kodesh (Holy Living Creatures or animals)

Auphanim The Wheels

Aralim The thrones

Chaschmalin The brilliant ones (In modern Hebrew the root word Chashmal means electricity)

Seraphim: The Fiery Ones

Melachim The Kings

Elohim The Gods. (This is the name God used when creating the earth in genesis. There is still much debate as to why God used a plural name for its self when it did so).

Beni Elohim: Sons of the Elohim

Kerubim The Cherubs

The Hebrew inscription on the outer edge is most appropriate for this seal. From Psalms 18:7 "

"Then the earth shook and trembled, the foundations of the hills also moved and were shaken, because He was wroth."

Day of week: Saturn

Candle Color: Black

We will discuss how to charge it and use it in the coming chapters.

The First Pentacle of Jupiter

A Talisman for acquiring more business as well as treasure.

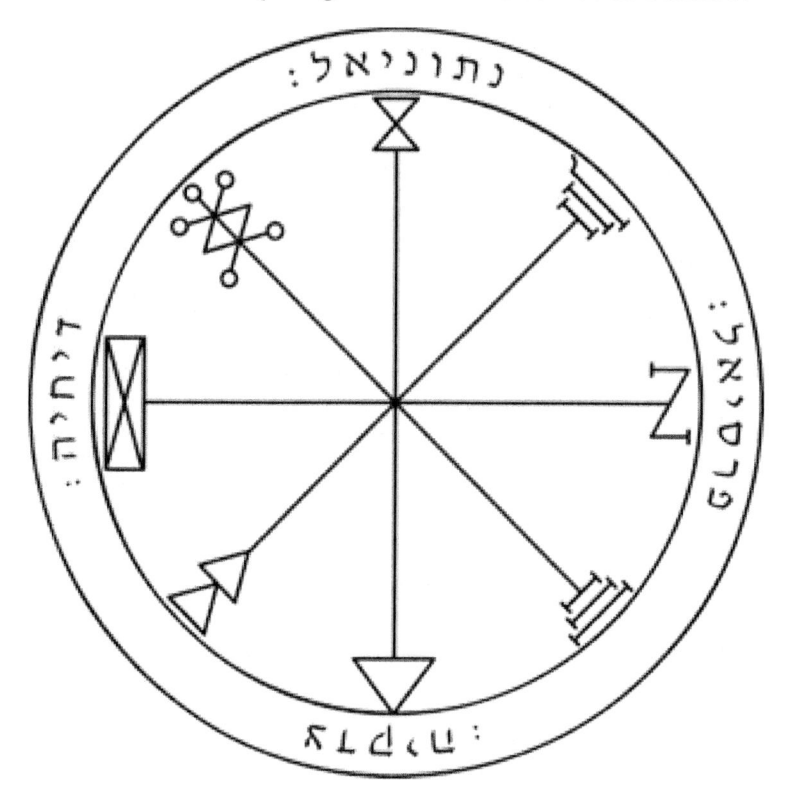

The Angelic names surrounding this seal are specific for the purpose of bringing in business and finding "treasure." They are from the top, counter clockwise.

Netoniel: This is an angel, who will help you achieve fame and notoriety.

Devachiah: he is the bestower of balance in all things and enhances a state of inner peace.

Tzedeqiah: Brings, riches, glory and honor.

Parasiel: He is the lord over vast treasures.

Day of week: Thursday

Candle Color: Gold

We will discuss how to charge it and use it in the coming chapters.

The Second Pentacle of Jupiter

This seal is used to acquire wealth and success.

The names of God in the Star of David are very power:

Aleph. Hey, Yod, Hey—Eh-ee-yeh

AB The father,

YHVH the four-letter name of God.

The biblical inscription is from Psalms 112:3

"Wealth and Riches are in his house, and his righteousness will endure forever."

Day of week: Thursday

Candle Color: Gold

We will discuss how to charge it and use it in the coming chapters.

The Third Pentacle of Jupiter

This Talisman is used for a general protection against spirits, whether you called upon them, others have, or they have come on their own.

The two Hebrew names of God at the center right are:

YHVH the four-letter name of God.

Aleph, Dalet, Noon, Yod Adonai.

The biblical inscription is from Psalms 125:1 "They that trust in the LORD shall be as mount Zion, which cannot be removed, but abide forever."

Day of week: Thursday

Candle Color: Black

We will discuss how to charge it and use it in the coming chapters.

The Fourth Pentacle of Jupiter

This like many other Jupiter seals is to bestow riches and honor on the person who carries it.

The Angelic names are:

Adoniel: This angel is used to increase luck in all things financial.

Bariel: Is the giver of long life and health.

The Inscription is from Psalms 112: 3" Wealth and riches shall be in his house: and his righteousness endures for ever."

Day of week: Thursday

Candle Color: Gold

We will discuss how to charge it and use it in the coming chapters.

The Fifth Pentacle of Jupiter

There is a legend that Joseph used this to attain his vision of the ladder that ascended to heaven. This Talisman will enhance your psychic visions and psychic abilities in general.

The letters within the talisman are combining to form certain Mystical Names of God.

The Biblical inscription is from Ezekiel 1:1 "...while I was among the exiles by the Kebar River, the heavens were opened, and I saw visions of God."

Day of week: Thursday

Candle Color: Purple

We will discuss how to charge it and use it in the coming chapters.

The Sixth Pentacle of Jupiter

This Seal is used to protect you from bodily harm.

The Angelic names are in the center and are:

Serph: which is from the order of angels which means fiery ones.

Kerub: which is from the order of the cherubim angels

Ariel: The lion of god and protector angel as well as one for new beginnings.

Tharsis: This angel is one of life choices and decision making. He can help you avoid danger.

The Hebrew inscription in the talisman is not from the bible, but it is translated. "They pierced my hands and my feet, I may tell all my bones." - Psalm 22:16

Day of week: Thursday

Candle Color: Black

We will discuss how to charge it and use it in the coming chapters.

The Seventh Pentacle of Jupiter

This Talisman is used to avoid and protect against poverty and financial hardship.

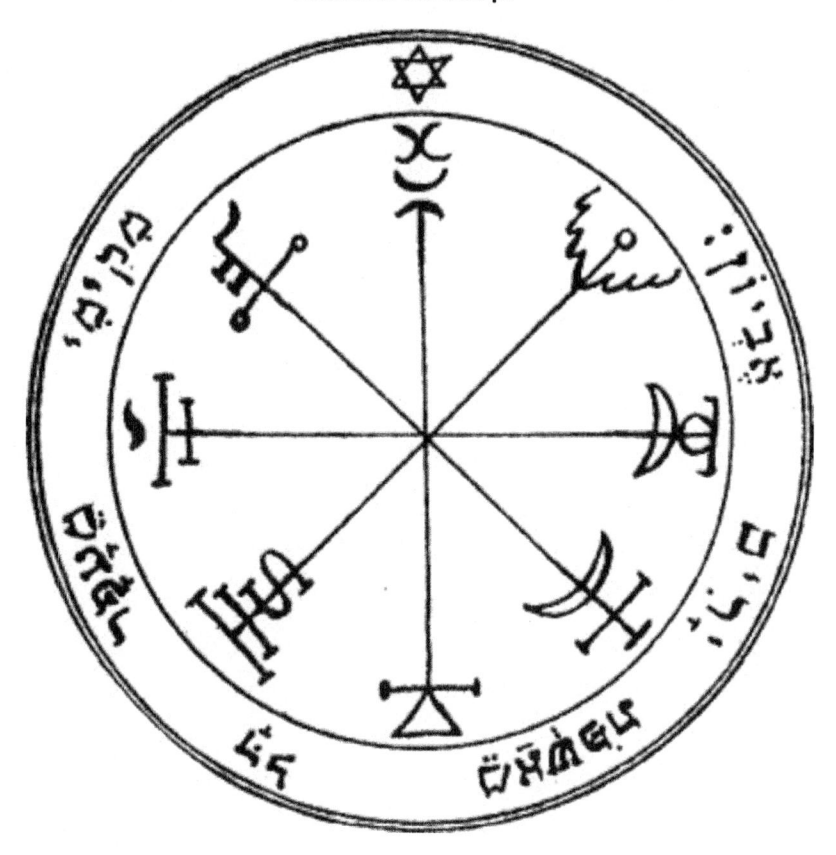

The Hebrew inscription around it says, "Lifting up the poor out of the mire, and raising the needy from the dunghill, that he may set him with princes, even with the princes of his people." — Psalms 113:7

Day of week: Thursday

Candle Color: Gold

We will discuss how to charge it and use it in the coming chapters.

The First Pentacle of Mars

The Talisman can be used to gain ambition, enthusiasm as well as courage.

The angelic names starting from the top and running counterclockwise are:

Madimiel: This angel vanquishes poverty, hunger and fear.

Bartzachiah: This angel helps from attain your ambitions without overdoing it.

Eschiel: This angel prevents one from becoming addicted to power but has also helped people fight addictions to substances as well.

Ithuriel: This angel works very much like the angel above. He is also quite famous and appears in John Milton's paradise lost.

Day of week: Tuesday

Candle Color: Red

We will discuss how to charge it and use it in the coming chapters.

The Second Pentacle of Mars

This is a great healing Talisman. The best way to use it is to apply it to the area that needs healing.

One of the names contained in this Talisman is up for debate. The name Joshua could also be Jesus. However, the verse that surrounds the talisman is from the book of John, so I am assuming it is Jesus. This is one of the more overtly christianized talisman. It doesn't make it less effective; it is just not in full alignment with the Solomonic traditions. The other names are YHVH the four-letter name of God and Elohim another name of god that is used in the book of Genesis.

The biblical reference is from John 1:4 "In Him was life, and the life was the light of man." - John 1:4

Day of week: Tuesday

Candle Color: Blue

We will discuss how to charge it and use it in the coming chapters.

The Third Pentacle of Mars

To incite hostility and discord wherever and to whomever you wish. It will also protect you from the ill intentions of others.

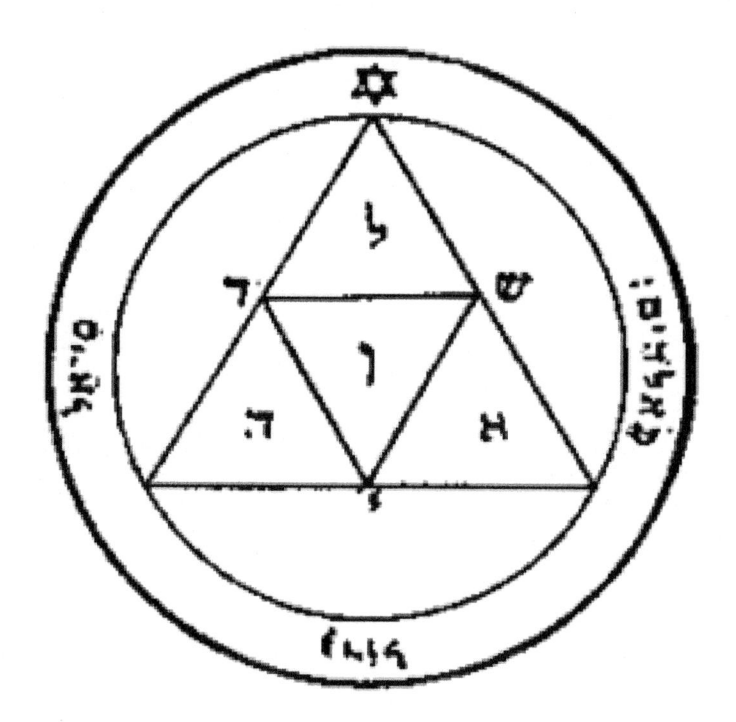

The names contained in the talisman are two powerful names of God.

El Shaddai and Eloah

The biblical verse is from Pslams 77:13: "Who is so great a God as our God?"

Day of week: Tuesday

Candle Color: Black

We will discuss how to charge it and use it in the coming chapters.

The Fourth Pentacle of Mars

This was historically used to grant victory in war. You can apply this to one's own life if you have an enemy you want to conquer.

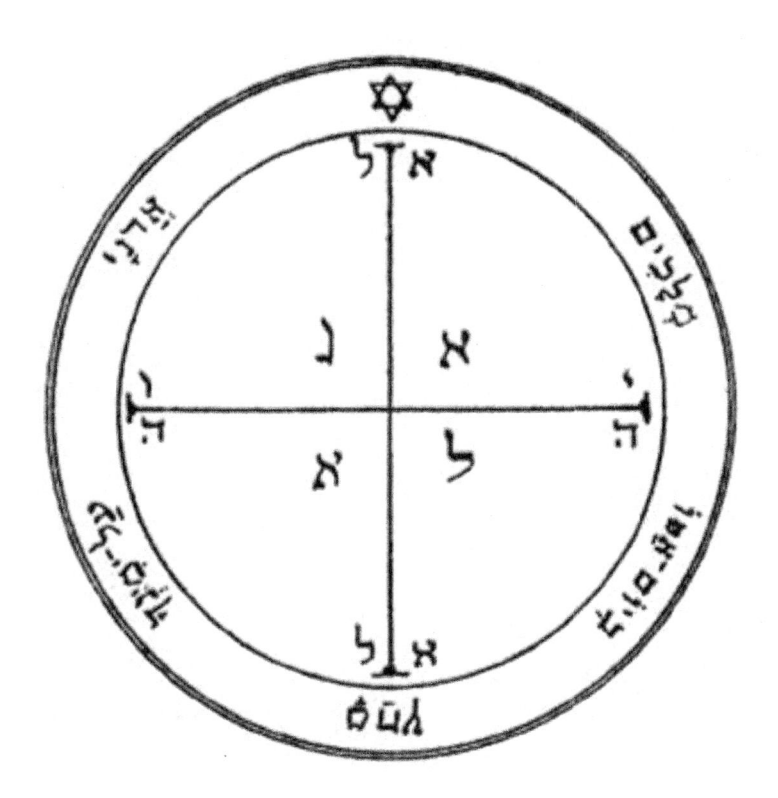

The Hebrew names are the three names of God. Agla, YHVH and EL.

The biblical verse is: "The Lord at thy right hand shall wound even Kings in the day of His Wrath." - Psalm 110:5

Day of week: Tuesday

Candle Color: Red

We will discuss how to charge it and use it in the coming chapters.

The Fifth Pentacle of Mars

This is a talisman that you can use when you are doing any kind of demonic binding. It will help you gain more control over the entity.

The Hebrew letters say HOL, it is not clear what this means.

The biblical inscription is from Psalms 91:13 "Thou shalt go upon the lion and added, the young lion and the dragon shalt thou tread under thy feet."

Day of week: Tuesday

Candle Color: Black

We will discuss how to charge it and use it in the coming chapters.

The Sixth Pentacle of Mars

If you have people who want to harm you, using this talisman will prevent harm from coming to you and will reverse their evil ways upon them.

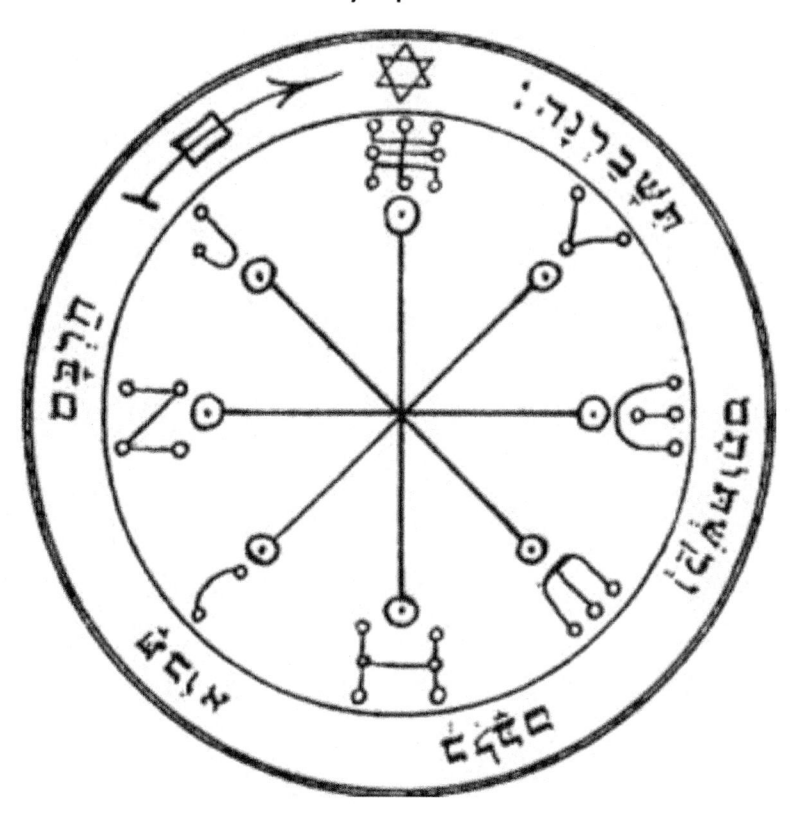

The biblical quote is: Psalm 37:15 "Their sword shall enter into their own heart, and their bow shall be broken."

Day of week: Tuesday

Candle Color: Black

We will discuss how to charge it and use it in the coming chapters.

The Seventh Pentacle of Mars

Another one that is interesting, it is used to control the weather through demonic forces. Perhaps we can use them on the enemies of the world?

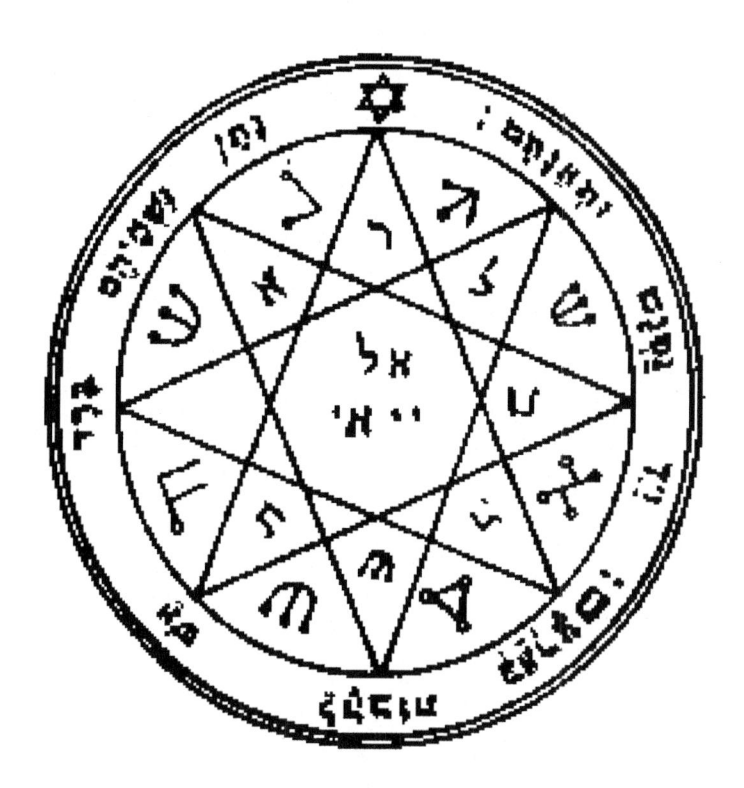

Hebrew Names of God: El and Yee ay

The Hebrew verse is from Psalms 105: 32-33: "He gave them hail for rain, and flaming fire in their land. He smote their vines also, and their fig-trees."

Day of week: Tuesday

Candle Color: Red AND black

We will discuss how to charge it and use it in the coming chapters.

The First Pentacle of the Sun

To gain control over all sentient beings as well as angelic beings for whatever purpose you wish.

Hebrew name of god is: El Shaddai

As a quick note, many think that horns are protruding from this image. In fact, it is divine ray of lights.

The latin inscription is "Behold His face and form by whom all things were made, and Whom all creatures obey."

Day of week: Sunday

Candle Color: Orange

We will discuss how to charge it and use it in the coming chapters.

The Second Pentacle of the Sun

To repress those who are haughty and arrogant in your presence and oppose your will.

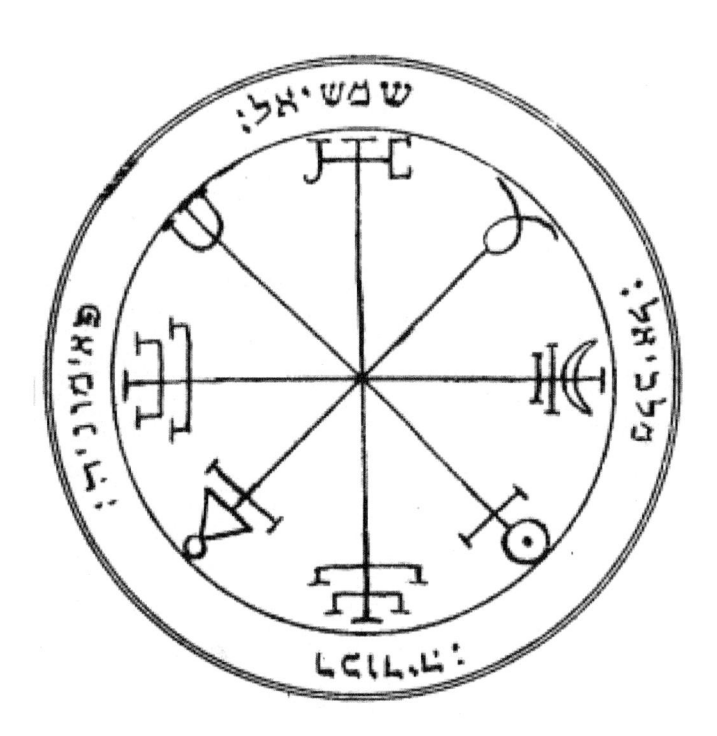

Angelic Names surrounding the Seal are counter clockwise:

Shemeshiel is the great angel who bears the knowledge and power of the sun

Paimoniah is an angel, who will humble individuals before you.

Rekhodiah this angel too is very powerful in manipulation and subjugation of individuals to your will.

Melkhiel this angel grants blessings, boons also bestows healings.

Day of week: Sunday

Candle Color: Orange

We will discuss how to charge it and use it in the coming chapters.

The Third Pentacle of the Sun

This Talisman is used to increase extreme wealth and entrepreneurship. This can also inflict losses on the people you deem your enemy or competition.

The Names within the talisman are the four-letter name of God appearing 21 times. The name is YHVH.

The Biblical inscription is from Daniel 4:34 "My Kingdom is an everlasting Kingdom, and my dominion endures from age to age."

Day of week: Sunday

Candle Color: Orange

We will discuss how to charge it and use it in the coming chapters.

The Fourth Pentacle of the Sun

This Talisman will allow you to see spirits of all kinds wherever you go.

The names of God are at the very center of the talisman. The names are YHVH and Adonai.

The biblical verse is from Psalms 33:3-4 "Lighten mine eyes that I sleep not in death, lest mine enemy say, I have prevailed against him."

Day of week: Sunday

Candle Color: Orange

We will discuss how to charge it and use it in the coming chapters.

The Fifth Pentacle of the Sun

Historically, this talisman has been used to traverse great distances in a short period of time.

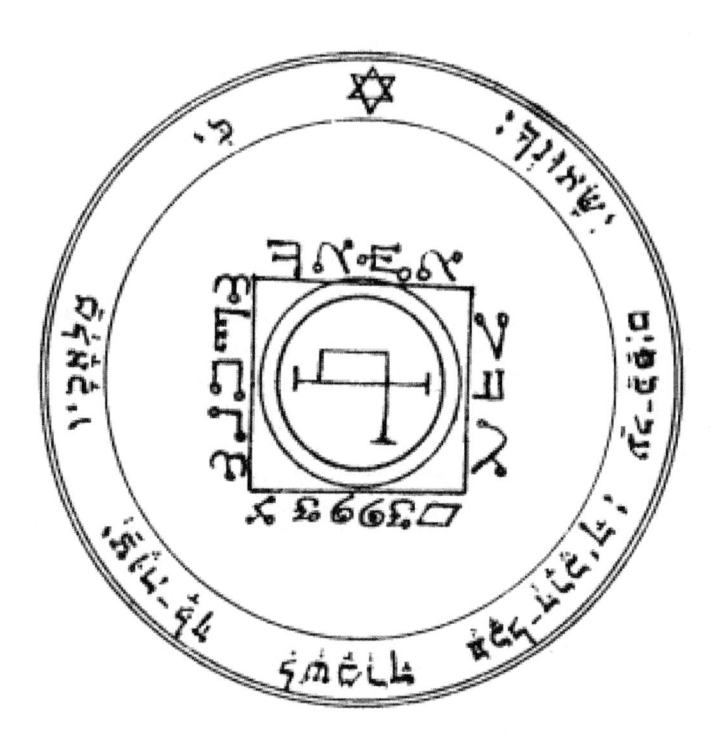

The biblical inscription is from Psalms 91:11-12: "He shall give His Angels charge over thee, to keep thee in all thy ways. They shall bear thee up in their hands."

Day of week: Sunday

Candle Color: Orange

We will discuss how to charge it and use it in the coming chapters.

The Sixth Pentacle of the Sun

This Talisman has been used to confer invisibility. I am not sure it works in the way that one might think. I feel this is a talisman that will make you go unnoticed, especially for you do not want to be noticed in a crowd or at an event. If you want to avoid a certain person or people, this is the talisman I feel will work for you.

The Biblical text is from Psalms 69:23 and 135:16: "Let their eyes be darkened that they see not; and make their loins continually to shake. They have eyes and see not."

Day of week: Sunday

Candle Color: Orange

We will discuss how to charge it and use it in the coming chapters.

The Seventh Pentacle of the Sun

If you feel you are imprisoned in your life or in a situation, this talisman is for you.

The angels within the talisman are:

Chasan, Angel of Air

Arel, Angel of Fire

Phorlakh, Angel of Earth;

Taliahad, Angel of water

The names of the four rulers of the Elements:

Serph: which is from the order of angels which means fiery ones.

Kerub: which is from the order of the cherubim angels

Ariel: The lion of god and protector angel as well as one for new beginnings.

Tharsis: This angel is one of life choices and decision making. He can help you avoid danger.

The Biblical Inscription is from Psalms 116:16-17: "Thou hast broken my bonds in sunder. I will offer unto thee the sacrifice of Thanksgiving, and will call upon the Name of Jehovah."

Day of week: Sunday

Candle Color: Orange

We will discuss how to charge it and use it in the coming chapters.

The First Pentacle of Venus

This Talisman will help you gain new friends, but also gain the lust and love of a certain person or persons.

The Angelic Names around the talisman are:

Nogahiel, this angel can help people to fall in love with you.

Acheliah, this angel inspires lust in others for you.

Socodiah (or Socohiah) this angel will give you courage in matters of love and interpersonal relationships.

Nangariel. This angel will help you not to get lost in obsessions about people you are trying to attract, keeping you more in control.

Day of week: Friday

Candle Color: Pink and or red

We will discuss how to charge it and use it in the coming chapters.

The Second Pentacle of Venus

This will help you to obtain grace & honor, and it will help you to accomplish all desires of the heart.

The biblical verse is from the Song of Solomon 8:6 "Place me as a signet upon thine heart, as a signet upon thine arm, for love is strong as death."

Day of week: Friday

Candle Color: Pink and or red

We will discuss how to charge it and use it in the coming chapters.

The Third Pentacle of Venus

This Talisman is supposedly so powerful that if you just show it to the person you want; they will be attracted to you and want to be with you.

The Names of God in the talisman are: YHVH and Adonai.

The Angelic names in the talisman are:

Ruach: Which means holy spirit.

Achides: Not much is known about this angel.

Aegalmiel, Not much is known about this angel.

Monachiel: This is an angel of love and romance.

Degaliel Not much is known about this angel.

The Biblical verse is from Genesis 1: 28: "And the Elohim blessed them, and the Elohim said unto them, 'Be ye fruitful, and multiply, and replenish the earth, and subdue it."

Day of week: Friday

Candle Color: Pink and or red

We will discuss how to charge it and use it in the coming chapters.

The Fourth Pentacle of Venus

This forces any person you want to get attracted to you.

The main name of God in this talisman is YHVH the powerful four letter name of God.

The biblical inscription is from Genesis 2:23-24

"This is bone of my bones, and flesh of my flesh. And they two were one flesh."

Day of week: Friday

Candle Color: Pink and or red

We will discuss how to charge it and use it in the coming chapters.

The Fifth Pentacle of Venus

Used to cause love and attraction in another person upon showing it to them, very similar to a previous talisman.

The biblical inscription is from Psalms 22:14 "My heart is like wax; it is melted in the midst of my bowels."

Day of week: Friday

Candle Color: Pink and or red

We will discuss how to charge it and use it in the coming chapters.

The First Pentacle of Mercury

This Talisman is used to increase your personal magnetism.

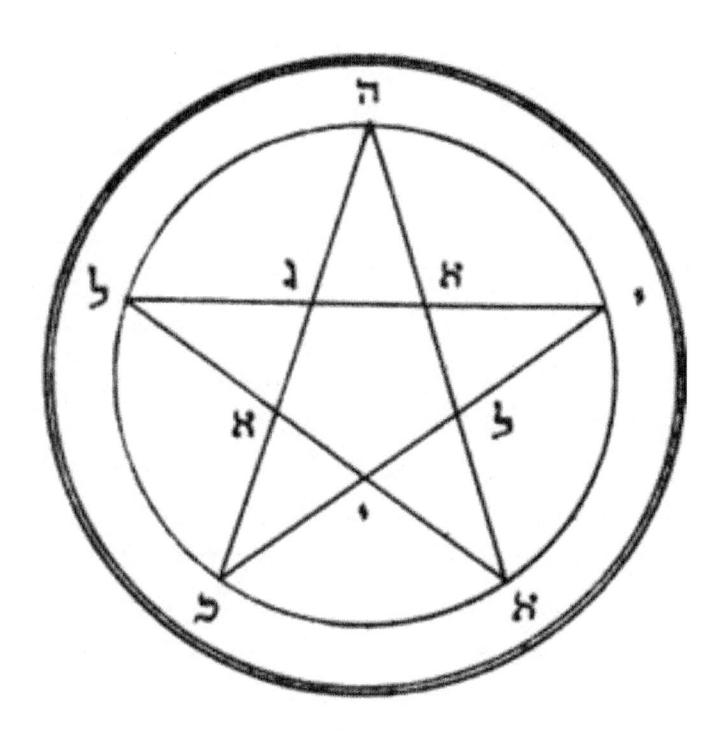

Angelic names are:

Yekahel: Not much is known about this angel other than he is one of the powers of this talisman.

Agiel: Same for this one, not much is known aside from his association with this talisman.

Day of week: Wednesday

Candle Color: Yellow

We will discuss how to charge it and use it in the coming chapters.

The Second Pentacle of Mercury

This is a wish-fulfillment talisman and is often used for wishes that seem almost impossible to achieve.

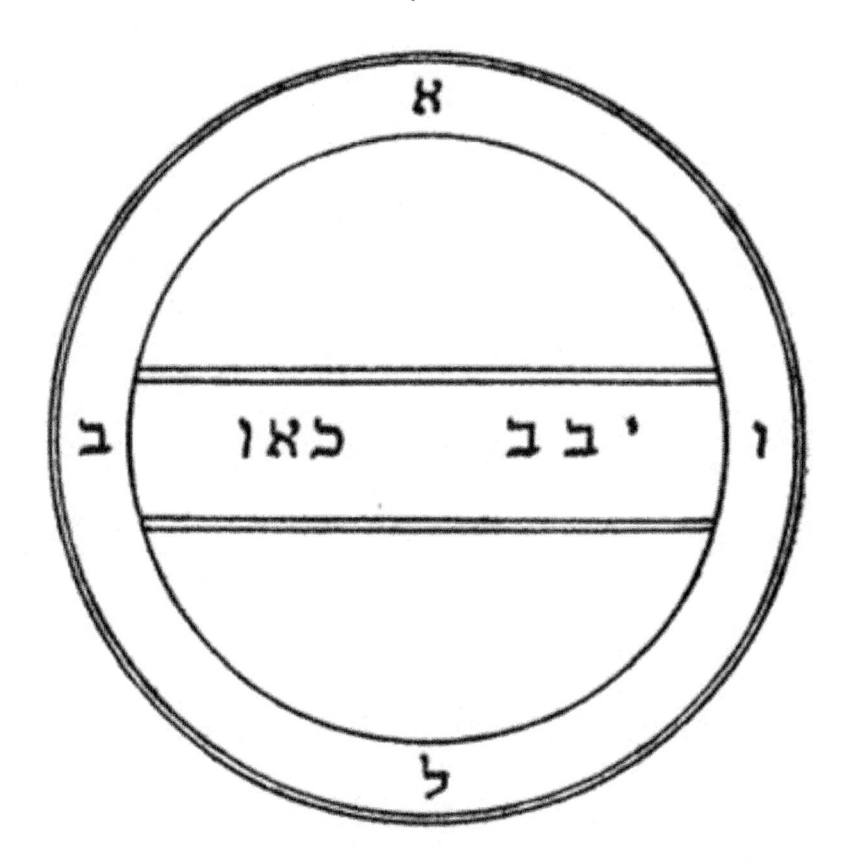

The Angelic name is:

Boel: He is one of the most exalted angels and has dominion over the four corners of the earth. This means that he can achieve anything.

Day of week: Wednesday

Candle Color: Yellow

We will discuss how to charge it and use it in the coming chapters.

The Third Pentacle of Mercury

If you are a writer or one who wishes to increase your writing and literary skills, this talisman is a very powerful one that will come in very handy for these endeavors.

Angelic Names are:

Kokaviel, this angel grants knowledge of science and magick, and some would say alchemy as well.

Gheoriah is a wonderful angel who helps you learn the deep mysteries of the spirit.

Savaniah very much the same as Gheoriah

Hokmahiel is a great angel, and his name means the wisdom of God. He can also bestow upon you great literally skills.

Day of week: Wednesday

Candle Color: Yellow

We will discuss how to charge it and use it in the coming chapters.

The Fourth Pentacle of Mercury

This will assist you in gaining knowledge and also understanding in any topic you wish. It will also help you discern the thoughts of others.

The Latin inscription is "Wisdom and virtue are in his house, and the Knowledge of all things remains with him forever."

The Hebrew words: EL (A Name of God); the following verse "God, fix Thou the Volatile, and let there be unto the void restriction."

Day of week: Wednesday

Candle Color: Yellow

We will discuss how to charge it and use it in the coming chapters.

The Fifth Pentacle of Mercury

It serves to open doors and portals of any kind, be it spiritual or physical, no barrier is too great for its power.

The Hebrew names of God are:

El a name of God; Ab which means father; and the four-letter name of God YHVH.

The biblical inscription is from Psalms 24:7: "Lift up your heads, O ye gates, and be ye lift up ye everlasting doors, and the King of Glory shall come in."

Day of week: Wednesday

Candle Color: Yellow

We will discuss how to charge it and use it in the coming chapters.

The First Pentacle of the Moon

This talisman is used to open doors both spiritually and earthly doors. It may not appear automatic, but it will guide you as to how to open them.

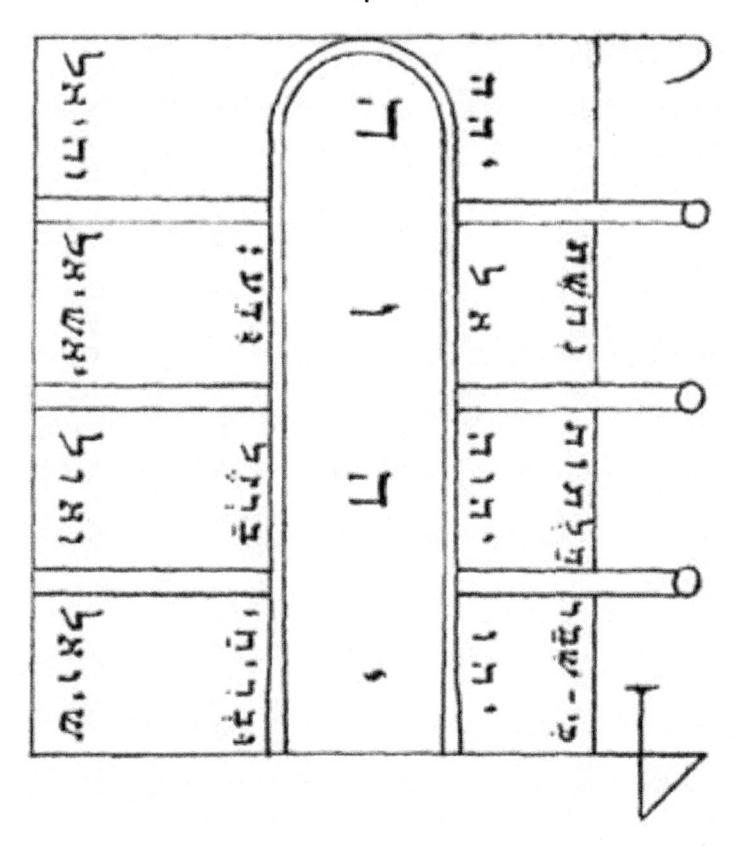

The Hebrew names of God are: YHVH, AL and variants of the YHVH.

The angelic names around the seal are:

Schioel: This angel is generally used to help with law suits and grants various legal protections.

Vaol: It Helps cultivate various kinds of creative talents as well as a bestower of success in general.

Yashiel: A good angel for all business endeavors.

Vehiel: This angel has been historically used to allow one to achieve astral projection.

The Biblical inscription is from Psalms 107:16: "He hath broken the Gates of brass, and smitten the bars of iron in sunder."

Day of week: Monday

Candle Color: Silver

We will discuss how to charge it and use it in the coming chapters.

The Second Pentacle of the Moon

This is used to protect you from every manner of natural disaster.

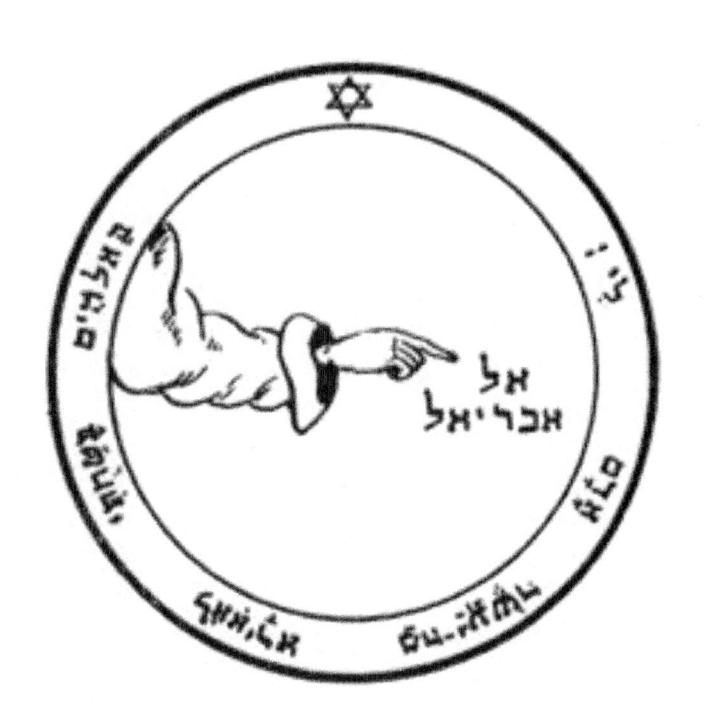

The name of God in the seal is: EL

The Angelic name under the name of God is:

Abariel: It is not clear what purpose this angel serves other than to help one invoke other spirits. However, coupled with the Name of God El it appears it services as protection against natural disasters.

The Biblical verse is from Psalms 56:11: "In Elohim, have I put my trust, I will not fear, what can man do unto me?"

Day of week: Monday

Candle Color: Silver

We will discuss how to charge it and use it in the coming chapters.

The Third Pentacle of the Moon

This seal is used to protect you from all things that go bump in the night. It Furthermore, protects one when traveling.

The Angelic Names are:

Aub

Vevaphel

These angels help protect and banish evil entities from entering your life in your sleep as well as when you are in your day to day. They can also bestow sacred and spiritual knowledge.

The biblical inscription is from Psalms 40:13 "Be pleased O God to deliver me, O God make haste to help me."

Day of week: Monday

Candle Color: Silver

We will discuss how to charge it and use it in the coming chapters.

The Fourth Pentacle of the Moon

This talisman is used for protection of every manner of evil. It can also be used to gain knowledge of herbs and stones.

The name of God within the seal is Eheieh Asher Eheieh, which means; I will be what I will be.

The angels associated with this seal are:

Yahel grants the knowledge of mystical wisdom, and the giving of mystical and magical power that the prophets once had.

Sofiel bestows knowledge of herbs, stones, and animal spirits; he can help you gain wisdom of all things nature. He is also wonderful at helping consecrate talisman.

The Latin inscription says, "Let them be confounded who persecute me, and let me not be confounded; let them fear, and not I"

Day of week: Monday

Candle Color: Silver

We will discuss how to charge it and use it in the coming chapters.

The Fifth Pentacle of the Moon

This is a great talisman to put under your pillow to get answers in your dreams. I have tried this one a few months ago, and I can attest to the usefulness of this one.

This seal can also be used to destroy your enemies and banish unwanted spiritual visitors.

The Hebrew names of God are:

YHVH and Elohim, the two most power names in the Old Testament.

The Angelic Names are:

Iachadiel: This angel will help you banish unwanted spiritual visitors; he is also known to help with the summoning o the dead.

Azarel: This angel can help you acquire special power to contact the spirit world to help provide answers in your dreams.

The Biblical inscription is from Psalms 68:1 "Let God arise, and let His enemies be scattered; let them also who hate him flee before Him."

Day of week: Monday

Candle Color: Silver

We will discuss how to charge it and use it in the coming chapters.

The Sixth Pentacle of the Moon

It is said that this Talisman can allow you to manipulate the weather as to cause heavy rains to come forth. Supposedly, if you keep this in water, the rain will continue until it is taken out.

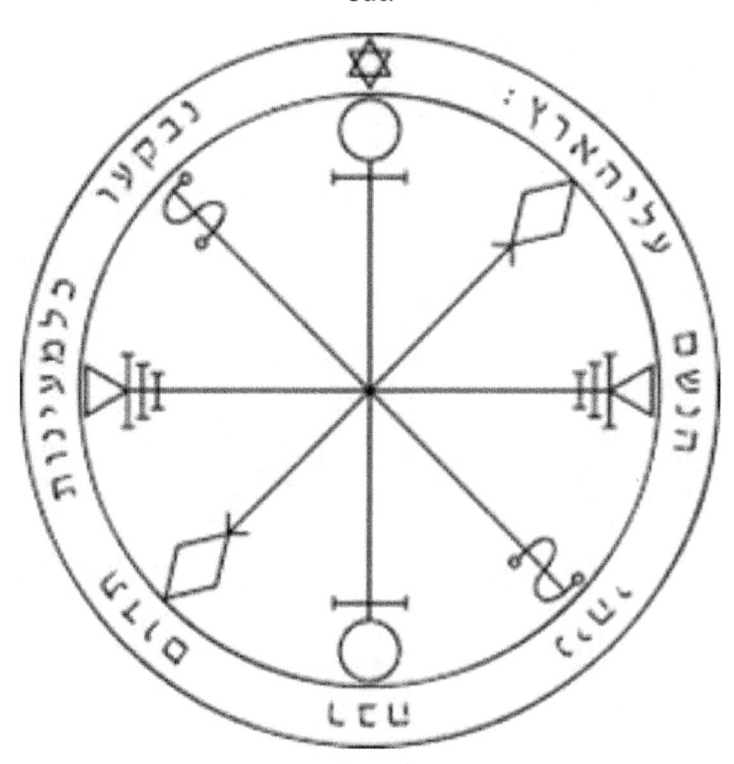

The Biblical verse is from Genesis 7: 11-12 " All the fountains of the great deep were broken up... and the rain was upon the earth."

Day of week: Monday

Candle Color: Silver

We will discuss how to charge it and use it in the coming chapters.

As you can see, there are 44 Talismans of Solomon, each with its own purpose. Many do overlap, and many contain angelic names who seem incongruent to their magickal purposes. Why this is, is not clear but throughout the centuries, people have used these seals with great success and like anything, if it is used, develops a kind of power, which compounds over time. That alone will bring about its supposed purpose. These are not the only seals; There are other seals of Solomon, some from Muslim sources. In a bonus of the book, I will display a few of these seals, but I will not go into great depth as to what magickal purposes they are used for. Now we will move on to what you will need for the rituals that I will present in this book.

What You Will Need for Talismanic Magick

In this brief chapter, we will discuss what you will need to perform the Talismanic magick in this book.

1. The Talisman: You will need the Talisman that you want to work with. Although you can technically print out an image; I would highly suggest getting one made of metal. I highly recommend James Hunter-Ralston's work. He can make one custom for you. You can reach him by email jhr922@yahoo.com or you can contact him via facebook page https://www.facebook.com/TheTalimancer

2. A Sage Smudge Stick: Although I do not mention smudge sticks very often, I do use them in my practice. They come in very handy when cleansing not only your space but any talisman or crystal you might be using. I recommend: White Sage Smudge 4" Sticks (pack of 3)

3. Frankincense and Myrrh: This Incense is a wonderful sacred fragrance and was once more precious than gold. It was so valuable that people would rather it than gold itself. I find the fragrance holy and fitting for this work. Frankincense and Myrrh

4. (Please note you can buy any kind of candle you like; they don't have to be chimes or votive. I just happen to like the ones I provided here) The candle colors are links to Amazon.

Red Chime Candles

Gold Candles.

Silver candles

Blue Candles:

Black Candles

Purple Candles

Orange

Pink

Yellow

5.	A piece of plain paper and a pen

6.	OPTIONAL: A bible: Most of the talismans are attached to biblical verses. However, I supply those verses for you each ritual and talisman.

As you can see you do not need many items. Of course, you do not need all the candles since you may not be working with all the talismans, but they are good to have in the event you do want to use more than one talisman, which will be a topic I will cover in the next chapter.

Charging and Using a Talisman

Before you use a talisman, whether it is made of metal or paper, it will need to be charged, perhaps cleansed is the right word. We do this because we want to "reset" the talisman so the energy is the talismans and yours and no one else's. Even paper can hold energy, and you want to make sure you are clear. You only need to charge the Talisman ONCE per ritual, not every time you use it. So if you repeat a ritual, your first charging is all that is needed.

I would also like to mention that using more than two Talismans at once. There are two reasons for this.

1.   Talisman, although they have their own intrinsic power, YOUR energy is needed as well and so if you have too many talismans working, you will lose that focused energy that you need to make it work.

2.   On a more practical level, if you use too many talismans, you won't know which one is working for you and, which is not. You will find that some talisman may not work for you. That is why I generally discourage more than two types of magick for a given purpose, as a magician you also want to know what works and what doesn't for you. It's very important to know this information. Only when I kept track did I know what worked for me.

Steps to Charging:

You will notice that the charging process is generic and not specific to the talisman, this is fine because now you are just cleansing it. We will be more specific when we get into the rituals.

1. Light the frankincense and Pass the talisman through the smoke.

2. Place the talisman at the center of the Altar

3. Take a piece of paper large enough to wrap it around the talisman. Write the intention you want for the talisman on this piece of paper and then wrap the talisman in the paper. You may also write symbols on the paper as well, any symbols you resonate with.

4. Sit for a moment and visualize the intention and "see" in your mind that energy is emanating from you and into the talisman that is wrapped in the paper.

5. Unwrap the talisman; pass it through the incense again.

6. Now hold the talisman and just sit with it for a moment.

7. Light the sage smudge stick and pass the smoke over the talisman and smudge yourself as well.

And that is all there is to it. No need for long drawn-out rituals. Although I recommend this simpler charging, you can certainly use anyone you wish, this happens to be the one I use.

In this next chapter, we will finally get to the rituals. For the sake of simplicity; each ritual will be a self-contained chapter, this way you can isolate the one that you want to perform a bit more efficiently. Let us begin.

Instructions

I will briefly go through the instructions, and then we will jump right into the 44 rituals.

1. Set up the Altar as such: The Talisman will always be in the middle. On the right side, place the candle/s. On the left place the Incense.

2. Charge the Talisman (Remember you only need to charge the Talisman ONCE per ritual not every time you use it. So if you repeat a ritual, your first charging is all that is needed.)

3. Light the candles

4. We will use the same incense we used to charge the talisman.

5. Pick up the talisman and place it your hands (Either hand or both)

6. Now sit in front of your altar and think about what it is you are using this talisman for. Once you have built a sufficient feeling and image of what it is you want.

7. Recite the words that are in the talisman three times (if applicable) (Out loud or to yourself.)

8. Invoke the angels or names of God of the talisman (I will supply the invocation) Do this once per angel/s. (Out loud or to yourself.)

9. Sit in silence and just feel the angels and or God. Visualize the power coming through the top of your head and out of your hands into the talisman. Watch it glow a side note, this can be a very powerful process)

10.   Place the Talisman down on the altar and thank the God/Angel if applicable for their assistance. I will supply a script. If no angel or name is assigned to a seal, this will be a general statement of affirmation.

11.   Leave the talisman on the Altar until the candle and incense are extinguished.

12.   When the candles and Incense have burned down, you are free to use the talisman how you please; you can wear it, put in your pocket or whatever is most appropriate for you based on the purpose of the talisman.

13.   As an added tip, from time to time imagine the light pulsating in the talisman, it will keep the energy in your mind.

That's pretty much it, it seems like many steps but all this can be done in a few minutes. In the next chapter, we will go through the rituals.

Ritual 1 – To Compel Others to do Your Will
First Pentacle of Saturn

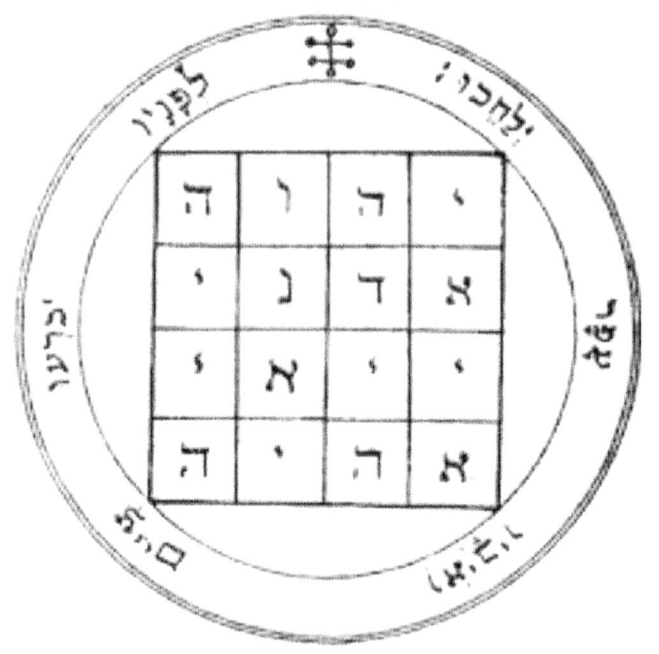

Ritual should be done On a Saturday

1. Setup the Altar as such: The Talisman will always be in the middle. On the right side, place the candle/s. On the left Place the Incense.

2. Charge the Talisman

3. Light the black candle

4. Light the incense

5. Pick up the talisman and place it your hands (Either hand or both)

6. Now sit in front of your altar and think about the person or persons you want to compel and how you want to compel them. Once you have built a sufficient feeling and image of what it is you want.

7. Recite the following verse with Conviction 'May the desert tribes bow before him and his enemies lick the dust."

8. Now Invoke the divine names as such: You, the most powerful and holy name Jehovah, with your power I compel _____ to do my bidding. You are Adonai the great lord and adon (lord) of all there is. I will be Adon over _____. I will be what I will be. Amen

9. Sit in silence and just feel the power of God coursing through you. Visualize the power coming though the top of your head and out of your hands into the talisman. Watch it glow.

10. Place the Talisman down and say "In gratitude I come before you Jehovah Adonai I know that you will grant this wish for me through this holy Talisman of Solomon Your servant.

11. Leave the talisman on the Altar until the candle and incense are extinguished.

12. When the candles and Incense have burned down, you are free to use the talisman how you please; you can wear it, put in your pocket or whatever is most appropriate for you based on the purpose of the talisman.

Ritual 2 – To Gain the Edge in any Competition
Second Pentacle of Saturn

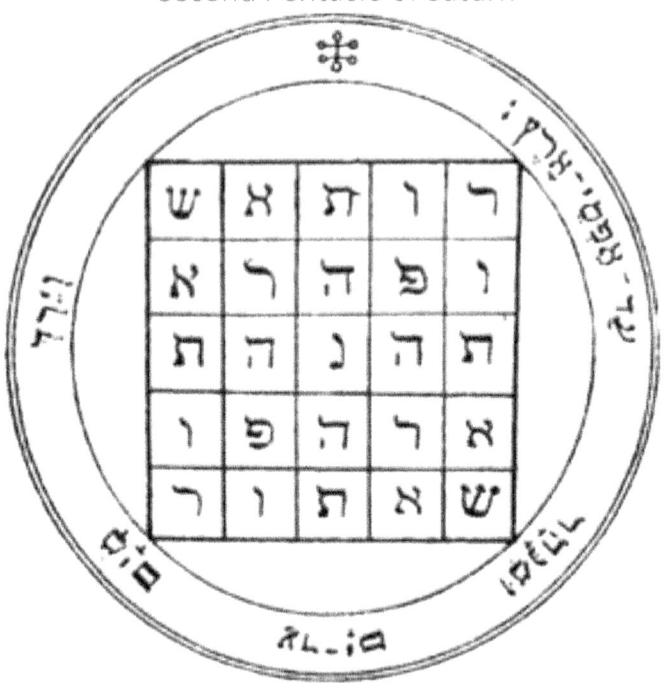

Ritual should be done On a Saturday

1. Setup the Altar as such: The Talisman will always be in the middle. On the right side, place the candle/s. On the left Place the Incense.

2. Charge the Talisman

3. Light the black candle

4. Light the incense

5. Pick up the talisman and place it your hands (Either hand or both)

6.   Now sit in front of your altar and think about the competition you are in and the edge you wish to gain from using the talisman. Once you have built a sufficient feeling and image of what it is you want.

7.   Recite the following verse with Conviction "May he rule from sea to sea and from the River to the ends of the earth."

8.   Since this talisman does not have holy names, look at the sacred square and its letters, just light gaze until the letters star to appear self-illuminated.

9.   Sit in silence and just feel the power of the talisman coursing through you. Visualize the power coming though the top of your head and out of your hands into the talisman. Watch it glow.

10.   Place the Talisman down and say "In the name of the almighty God, grant this wish for me through this holy Talisman of Solomon Your servant".

11.   Leave the talisman on the Altar until the candle and incense are extinguished.

12.   When the candles and Incense have burned down, you are free to use the talisman how you please; you can wear it, put in your pocket or whatever is most appropriate for you based on the purpose of the talisman.

Ritual 3 – To Defend Against Psychic Attacks of Others

Third Pentacle of Saturn

Ritual should be done On a Saturday

1. Setup the Altar as such: The Talisman will always be in the middle. On the right side, place the candle/s. On the left Place the Incense.

2. Charge the Talisman

3. Light the black candle

4. Light the incense

5. Pick up the talisman and place it your hands (Either hand or both)

6. Now sit in front of your altar and think about the person or persons that you suspect are psychically attacking OR you can think of just being protected from potential attacks.. Once you have built a sufficient feeling and image of what it is you want.

7. Now Invoke the angelic names as such: Oh Mighty angel Omliel I command you in the name of King Solomon your lord that you be bound to this seal and that you will protect me from the evil spirits my enemies cast upon me. So be it.

To you angel Anachiel I command you in the name of King Solomon your lord that you neutralize all my enemies before me. May they not be able to harm me in any way, I command you angel Anachiel HEAR ME.

You the Great Angel Arauchia the great revealer of truth I command you by the name of King Solomon and by this holy seal that you reveal and protect me from the people who wish to harm me.

You angel Anatzchia, I bind you to this seal in the name of King Solomon your master to protect me from all evils of others. So Mote it be.

8. Sit in silence and just feel the power of these angels coursing through you. Visualize the power coming though the top of your head and out of your hands into the talisman. Watch it glow.

9.   Place the Talisman down and say " Go you angels Omliel Anachiel Aruachia and Anatzchia and do my bidding and remember this holy seal in which I bind you. Amen

10.   Leave the talisman on the Altar until the candle and incense are extinguished.

11.   When the candles and Incense have burned down, you are free to use the talisman how you please; you can wear it, put in your pocket or whatever is most appropriate for you based on the purpose of the talisman.

Ritual 4 – To Destroy Your Enemies Totally

Please be careful with this one

Fourth Pentacle of Saturn

Ritual should be done On a Saturday

1. Setup the Altar as such: The Talisman will always be in the middle. On the right side, place the candle/s. On the left Place the Incense.

2. Charge the Talisman

3. Light the black candle

4. Light the incense

5. Pick up the talisman and place it your hands (Either hand or both)

6. Now sit in front of your altar and think about your enemy and what they have done to you, channel your anger and see what it is you want done to them. Once you have built a sufficient feeling and image of what it is you want.

7. Recite the following verses with Conviction "Hear, O Israel: The LORD our God, the LORD is one."" He wore cursing as his garment; it entered into his body like water, into his bones like oil."

8. Since this talisman does not have holy names, look at the center of the talisman and its letters, just light gaze until the letters star to appear self-illuminated.

9. Sit in silence and just feel the power of the talisman coursing through you. Visualize the power coming though the top of your head and out of your hands into the talisman. Watch it glow.

10. Place the Talisman down and say "In the name of the almighty God, grant that my enemy gets crushed by the help of this holy Talisman of Solomon The King".

11. Leave the talisman on the Altar until the candle and incense are extinguished.

12. When the candles and Incense have burned down, you are free to use the talisman how you please; you can wear it, put in your pocket or whatever is most appropriate for you based on the purpose of the talisman.

Ritual 5 – For General Protection
Fifth Pentacle of Saturn

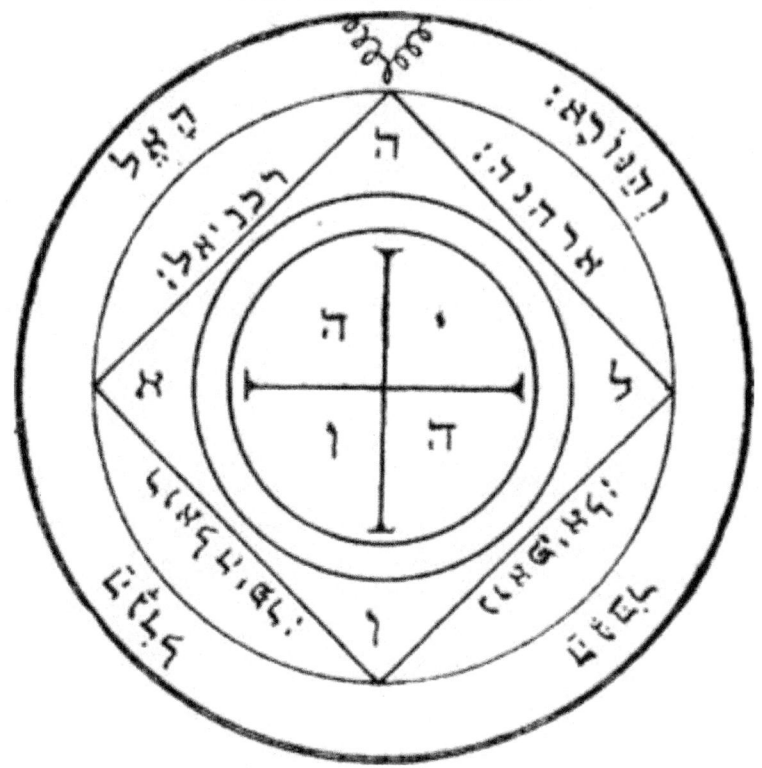

Ritual should be done On a Saturday

1. Setup the Altar as such: The Talisman will always be in the middle. On the right side, place the candle/s. On the left Place the Incense.

2. Charge the Talisman

3. Light the black candle

4. Light the incense

5. Pick up the talisman and place it your hands (Either hand or both)

6. Now sit in front of your altar and think about your need for either general protection from harm or for protection during a certain activity. Once you have built a sufficient feeling and image of what it is you want.

7. Recite the following verse with Conviction "For the LORD your God is God of gods and Lord of lords, the great God, mighty and awesome, who shows no partiality and accepts no bribes."

8. Now Invoke the divine names as such: You, the most powerful and holy name of Eloha Jehovah, with your power I as that you protect my comings and goings through this mighty seal of your servant King Solomon. Amen

9. Now Invoke the angels: Oh Benevolent angel Arehanah I ask and command you in the name of King Solomon your lord that you be my guide that I will remain safe and the choices I make will be made for my highest good. So be it By Eloha Jehovas name.

To you angel Rakhaniel I ask and command you in the name of King Solomon your lord that you also give me the wisdom to keep myself self and that if a situation or person is not good for me, that you will give me the foresight to remove myself from the situation or person. Hear Me Now!

You the Great Angel Roelhaiphar In the name of the almighty I ask you to protect me from all manner of danger and that tragedy will not befall me. In the name of this great seal, you will heed my call.

You angel Noaphiel, I bind you to this seal in the name of King Solomon your master to protect me So Mote it be.

10.   Sit in silence and just feel the power of God coursing through you. Visualize the power coming though the top of your head and out of your hands into the talisman. Watch it glow.

11.   Place the Talisman down and say "Go you angels of this mighty seal, go and protect me from all dangers that may come across my path, in the name of Eloha Jehovah. Amen

12.   Leave the talisman on the Altar until the candle and incense are extinguished.

13.   When the candles and Incense have burned down, you are free to use the talisman how you please; you can wear it, put in your pocket or whatever is most appropriate for you based on the purpose of the talisman.

Ritual 6 – To Send Your Enemies Ghosts, Poltergeist and Demons

Please Use With Caution

Sixth Pentacle of Saturn

Ritual should be done On a Saturday

1. Setup the Altar as such: The Talisman will always be in the middle. On the right side, place the candle/s. On the left Place the Incense.

2. Charge the Talisman

3. Light the black candle

4. Light the incense

5. Pick up the talisman and place it your hands (Either hand or both)

6. Now sit in front of your altar and think about your enemy, think of how you would desire a demon or ghost to come and haunt them. Sending a spirit to haunt an enemy is one of the best ways to defeat them. Once you have built a sufficient feeling and image of what it is you want.

7. Recite the following verse with Conviction "Set upon him a wicked one to be ruler over him, and let Satan stand at his right hand."

8. Since this talisman does not have holy names, look at the center of the talisman and its angelic letters, just light gaze until the letters star to appear self-illuminated.

9. Sit in silence and just feel the power of the talisman coursing through you. Visualize the power coming though the top of your head and out of your hands into the talisman. Watch it glow.

10. Place the Talisman down and say "In the name of King Solomon grant that my enemy will be plagued and haunted by spirits until they will are defeated".

11.   Leave the talisman on the Altar until the candle and incense are extinguished.

12.   When the candles and Incense have burned down, you are free to use the talisman how you please; you can wear it, put in your pocket or whatever is most appropriate for you based on the purpose of the talisman.

Ritual 7 – To Cause Earthquakes

Seventh Pentacle of Saturn

I am not sure why one would need this but this seal is to cause or worsen an earthquake.

Ritual should be done On a Saturday

1. Setup the Altar as such: The Talisman will always be in the middle. On the right side, place the candle/s. On the left Place the Incense.

2. Charge the Talisman

3. Light the black candle

4. Light the incense

5. Pick up the talisman and place it your hands (Either hand or both)

6. Now sit in front of your altar and think of where you would like an earthquake to occur (Not sure this is a wise move). Once you have built a sufficient feeling and image of what it is you want.

7. Recite the following verse with Conviction "Then the earth shook and trembled, the foundations of the hills also moved and were shaken, because He was wroth."

8. Now Invoke the order of angels within the seal:

Oh Most blessed Chayot Ha Kodesh I ask and command you in the name of King Solomon your lord that you Shake the earth asunder and cause those upon the earth to tremble deep in their souls

To you angel Auphanim I ask and command you in the name of King Solomon your lord that you also shake the land and case the hearts of man to fear me.

You the Great Chaschmalin In the name of the almighty I ask you to send lighting upon the earth that will crack the earth asunder and cause a rumbling so great that men will fear.

You the order of Seraphim, I bind you to this seal in the name of King Solomon your master that you will shake the earth with your splendor, strike the earth so that everyone will remember this day.

You the order of Aralim, I bind you to this seal that you may raise low the earth beneath _____ so as to cause an earth catastrophe that even the mighty will not recover from.

You the order of Melachim, Oh kings of the heaven and the earth. With your great might, smite the earth that it will tremble and that man will speak of your power.

You the order of Elohim, you who created the heaven and the earth, you who raised the earth from the great chaotic abyss, bring upon _____ an earthquake so mighty that none like it has ever been experienced in history. By the power of this seal a implore you.

You the order of Beni Elohim, the children of the God you who hath witnesses the heaven and the earth in creation, you who witnesses the earth emerge from the great chaotic abyss, bring upon _____ an earthquake that will be recounted for generations to come.

You the order of Kerubim, you of the great and powerful order, lay waste the land that no man will be able to walk upon it for generations to come. SO MOTE IT BE.

9. Sit in silence and just feel the power of God coursing through you. Visualize the power coming though the top of your head and out of your hands into the talisman. Watch it glow.

10. Place the Talisman down and say "Go you of the great angelic orders, go and do my bidding, shake the earth and the hearts of men in fear in the name of the great King Solomon. Amen

11. Leave the talisman on the Altar until the candle and incense are extinguished.

12. When the candles and Incense have burned down, you are free to use the talisman how you please; you can wear it, put in your pocket or whatever is most appropriate for you based on the purpose of the talisman.

Ritual 8 – To Increase Business Success
The First Pentacle of Jupiter

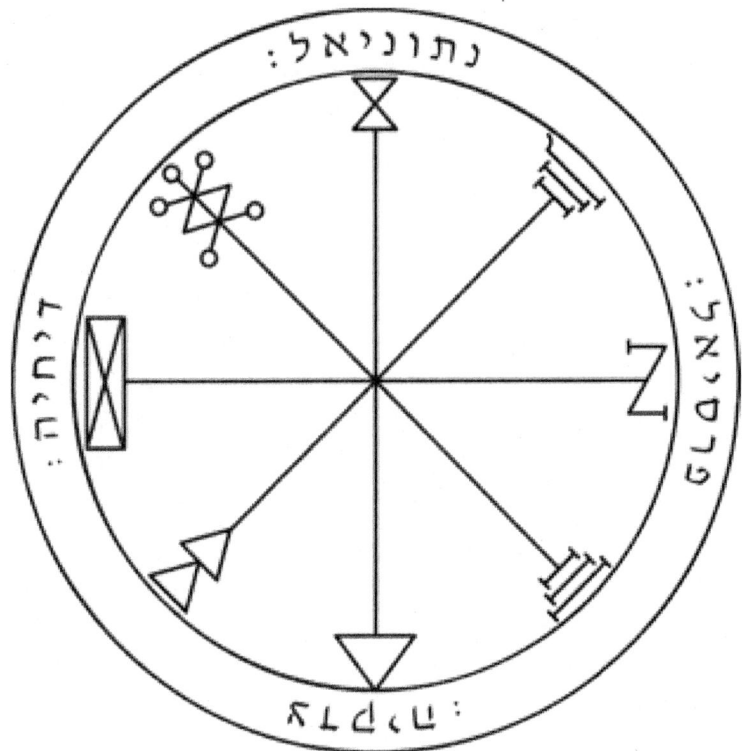

Ritual should be done On a Thursday

1. Setup the Altar as such: The Talisman will always be in the middle. On the right side, place the candle/s. On the left Place the Incense.

2. Charge the Talisman

3. Light the Gold candle

4. Light the incense

5. Pick up the talisman and place it your hands (Either hand or both)

6. Now sit in front of your altar and think about your need to bring in new business and extra income Once you have built a sufficient feeling and image of what it is you want.

7. Now Invoke the angels:

Oh Benevolent angel Netoniel I ask and command you in the name of King Solomon your lord that you bring me great wealth through my business. You are known to bring this quickly; I implore you by this seal that you do so.

To you angel Devachiah I ask and command you in the name of King Solomon your lord that you also give me more business but to also allow me to deal wisely in all my business dealings as well, by the power of ths mighty seal it will be done.

You the Great Angel Tzedeqiah In the name of the almighty God I ask you to make my business well known so I may have more than enough business to bring me great success, by the power and merit of King Solomon this will be done.

You angel Parasiel I bind you to this seal in the name of King Solomon your master so that my business will be a great success. You are wise in counsel and great in power, help me now!

8.   Sit in silence and just feel the power of God coursing through you. Visualize the power coming though the top of your head and out of your hands into the talisman. Watch it glow.

9.   Place the Talisman down and say "Go you angels of this mighty seal, go and bring forth abundance in the name of the great king Solomon who binds you. Amen

10.   Leave the talisman on the Altar until the candle and incense are extinguished.

11.   When the candles and Incense have burned down, you are free to use the talisman how you please; you can wear it, put in your pocket or whatever is most appropriate for you based on the purpose of the talisman.

Ritual 9 – To Acquire Wealth and Success
The Second Pentacle of Jupiter

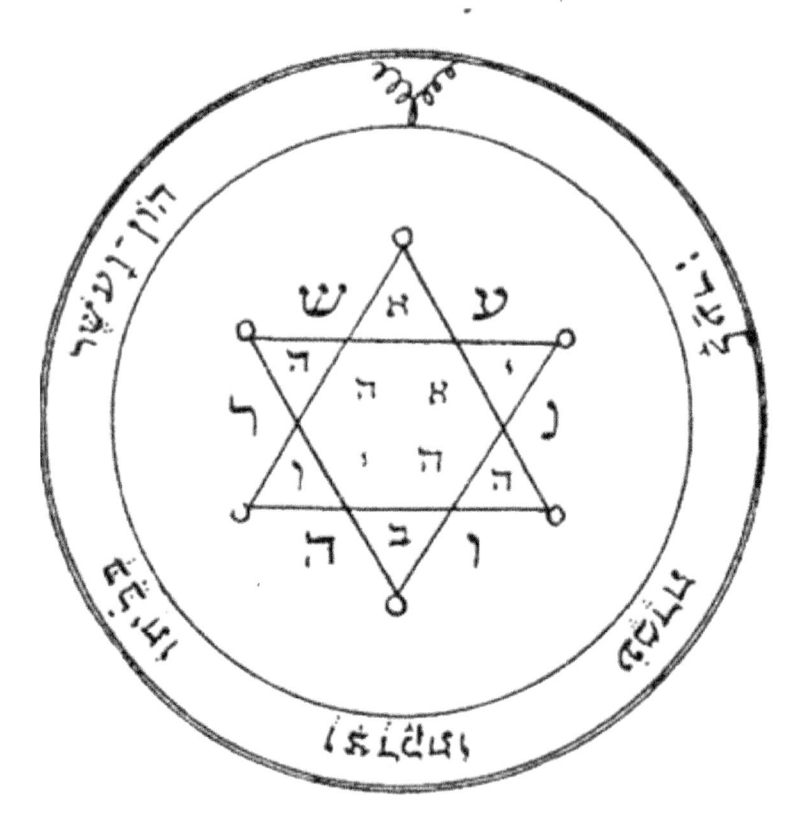

Ritual should be done On a Thursday

1. Setup the Altar as such: The Talisman will always be in the middle. On the right side, place the candle/s. On the left Place the Incense.

2. Charge the Talisman

3. Light the Gold candle

4. Light the incense

5. Pick up the talisman and place it your hands (Either hand or both)

6. Now sit in front of your altar and think about Acquiring great wealth and success in all that you do. Once you have built a sufficient feeling and image of what it is you want.

7. Recite the following verse with Conviction "Wealth and Riches are in his house, and his righteousness endures forever."

8. Now Invoke the divine names as such: You, the most powerful and holy name Jehovah – Ehieh, with your power I attract wealth and success to me. You are my AB the great lord and AB (Father) of all there is. I know you will bring me the prosperity that I request. Amen

9. Sit in silence and just feel the power of God coursing through you. Visualize the power coming though the top of your head and out of your hands into the talisman. Watch it glow.

10. Place the Talisman down and say "In gratitude I come before you Jehovah –Ehieh My father, I know that you will grant this wish for me through this holy Talisman of Solomon Your servant.

11. Leave the talisman on the Altar until the candle and incense are extinguished.

12. When the candles and Incense have burned down, you are free to use the talisman how you please; you can wear it, put in your pocket or whatever is most appropriate for you based on the purpose of the talisman.

Ritual 10 – To General Protection Against Spirits That Can Harm
The Third Pentacle of Jupiter

Ritual should be done On a Thursday

1. Setup the Altar as such: The Talisman will always be in the middle. On the right side, place the candle/s. On the left Place the Incense.

2. Charge the Talisman

3. Light the Black candle

4. Light the incense

5.   Pick up the talisman and place it your hands (Either hand or both)

6.   Now sit in front of your altar and think about your need for protection against spirits or a certain spirit you feel is inflicting harm on you. Once you have built a sufficient feeling and image of what it is you want.

7.   Recite the following verse with Conviction "They that trust in the LORD shall be as mount Zion, which cannot be removed, but abideth forever."

8.   Now Invoke the divine names as such: You, the most powerful and holy name Jehovah – Adonai, with your power I implore you to protect me from the spirits and entities that wish to harm me, by the power vested in this Seal, you will protect me. Amen

9.   Sit in silence and just feel the power of God coursing through you. Visualize the power coming though the top of your head and out of your hands into the talisman. Watch it glow.

10.   Place the Talisman down and say "In gratitude I come before you Jehovah –Adonai, The great protector, I know that you will grant this wish for me through this holy Talisman of Solomon Your servant.

11.   Leave the talisman on the Altar until the candle and incense are extinguished.

12.   When the candles and Incense have burned down, you are free to use the talisman how you please; you can wear it, put in your pocket or whatever is most appropriate for you based on the purpose of the talisman.

Ritual 11 – For the Acquisition of Great Wealth and Honor

The Fourth Pentacle of Jupiter

Ritual should be done On a Thursday

1. Setup the Altar as such: The Talisman will always be in the middle. On the right side, place the candle/s. On the left Place the Incense.

2. Charge the Talisman

3.   Light the Gold candle

4.   Light the incense

5.   Pick up the talisman and place it your hands (Either hand or both)

6.   Now sit in front of your altar and think about your desire for great Wealth and Honor. Once you have built a sufficient feeling and image of what it is you want.

7.   Recite the following verse with Conviction "Wealth and riches shall be in his house: and his righteousness endures forever."

8.   Now Invoke the Angelic names as such:

Oh Angel Adoniel, in the name of your great King Solomon I implore you to between unto me good fortune, good luck and prosperity. By this great seal I bind you.

You, Angel Bariel bestow unto me not only great riches and honor but the health and long life that will allow me to enjoy such wealth. In the Name of King Solomon your king, You are bound.

9.   Sit in silence and just feel the power of God coursing through you. Visualize the power coming though the top of your head and out of your hands into the talisman. Watch it glow.

10.   Place the Talisman down and say "In gratitude I come before angel Adoniel for listening to my request, in the name of

the Great King Solomon and God Almighty you will grant this request to me.

In great thanks I come before you angel Bariel for heading my call, in the name of your Master King Solomon and the God above you will grant my desires.

11.   Leave the talisman on the Altar until the candle and incense are extinguished.

12.   When the candles and Incense have burned down, you are free to use the talisman how you please; you can wear it, put in your pocket or whatever is most appropriate for you based on the purpose of the talisman

Ritual 12 – For Development of Psychic Powers
The Fifth Pentacle of Jupiter

Ritual should be done On a Thursday

1. Setup the Altar as such: The Talisman will always be in the middle. On the right side, place the candle/s. On the left Place the Incense.

2. Charge the Talisman

3. Light the Purple candle

4. Light the incense

5.   Pick up the talisman and place it your hands (Either hand or both)

6.   Now sit in front of your altar and think about your desire to increase and or develop psychic and Intuitive powers. Once you have built a sufficient feeling and image of what it is you want.

7.   Now Say the following verse with great conviction: "while I was among the exiles by the Kebar River, the heavens were opened and I saw visions of God."

8.   Sit in silence and just feel the power of God coursing through you. Visualize the power coming though the top of your head and out of your hands into the talisman. Watch it glow.

9.   Leave the talisman on the Altar until the candle and incense are extinguished.

10.   When the candles and Incense have burned down, you are free to use the talisman how you please; you can wear it, put in your pocket or whatever is most appropriate for you based on the purpose of the talisman.

Ritual 13 – For the Protection from Bodily Harm
The Sixth Pentacle of Jupiter

Ritual should be done On a Thursday

1. Setup the Altar as such: The Talisman will always be in the middle. On the right side, place the candle/s. On the left Place the Incense.

2. Charge the Talisman

3. Light the black candle

4. Light the incense

5. Pick up the talisman and place it your hands (Either hand or both)

6. Now sit in front of your altar and think of your need for physical safety, either day-to-day or if you are going om a trip and feel the need for protection. Once you have built a sufficient feeling and image of what it is you want.

7. Recite the following verse with Conviction "They pierced my hands and my feet, I may tell all my bones."

8. Now Invoke the order of angels and the 2 angels within the seal:

You the order of Seraphim, I bind you to this seal in the name of King Solomon your master that you will grant me the protection I need , do so now.

You the order of Kerubim, you of the great and powerful order, you who protect those who call upon you, guide me that I will not enter in harm of either body, mind and spirit.

Oh great angel Ariel, The lion of god protect me in all my ways. In the name of your King Solomon I bind you to this seal of protection.

In the name of the almighty and your master King Solomon, angel Tharsis I bind you to this Seal so that you may be my guide when I find myself in an unknown situation. Make my decisions wise and clear. I bind you to this seal, so mote it be.

9. Sit in silence and just feel the power of God coursing through you. Visualize the power coming though the top of your head and out of your hands into the talisman. Watch it glow.

10. Place the Talisman down and say "Go you of the great angelic orders, go and do my bidding, protect me from all harm in the name of the great King Solomon. Amen

11. Leave the talisman on the Altar until the candle and incense are extinguished.

12. When the candles and Incense have burned down, you are free to use the talisman how you please; you can wear it, put in your pocket or whatever is most appropriate for you based on the purpose of the talisman.

Ritual 14 – For the Protection Against Poverty and Financial Hardship
The Seventh Pentacle of Jupiter

Ritual should be done On a Thursday

1. Setup the Altar as such: The Talisman will always be in the middle. On the right side, place the candle/s. On the left Place the Incense.

2. Charge the Talisman

3. Light the Gold candle

4. Light the incense

5. Pick up the talisman and place it your hands (Either hand or both)

6. Now sit in front of your altar and think about acquiring enough money to avoid financial hardships that m ay occur unexpectedly. . Once you have built a sufficient feeling and image of what it is you want.

7. Recite the following verse with Conviction "Lifting up the poor out of the mire, and raising the needy from the dunghill, that he may set him with princes, even with the princes of his people."

8. Sit in silence and just feel the power of God coursing through you. Visualize the power coming though the top of your head and out of your hands into the talisman. Watch it glow.

9. Place the Talisman down and say "In gratitude I come before you Lord of the universe, I know that you will grant this wish for me through this holy Talisman of Solomon Your servant.

10. Leave the talisman on the Altar until the candle and incense are extinguished.

11. When the candles and Incense have burned down, you are free to use the talisman how you please; you can wear it, put in your pocket or whatever is most appropriate for you based on the purpose of the talisman.

Ritual 15 – To Gain Ambition, Enthusiasm and Courage
The First Pentacle of Mars

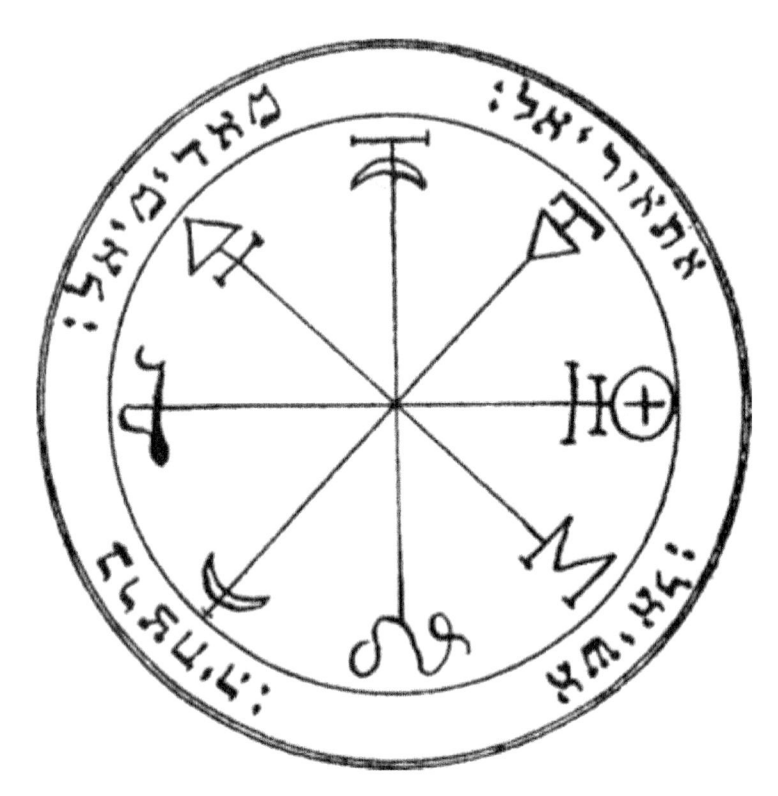

Ritual should be done On a Tuesday

1. Setup the Altar as such: The Talisman will always be in the middle. On the right side, place the candle/s. On the left Place the Incense.

2. Charge the Talisman

3. Light the Red candle

4. Light the incense

5.   Pick up the talisman and place it your hands (Either hand or both)

6.   Now sit in front of your altar and think about your need to gain more courage, confidence and enthusiasm. It could be a general request or for a particular event. Once you have built a sufficient feeling and image of what it is you want.

7.   Now Invoke the angels:

Oh Benevolent angel Madimiel I ask and command you in the name of King Solomon your lord that you make me fearless in the face of what I fear. You are known to bring this quickly; I implore you by this seal that you do so.

To you angel Bartzachiah I ask and command you in the name of King Solomon your lord that you also give me more ambition for I feel I am not able to move forward in life. In the name of Solomon make this so.

You the Great Angel Eschiel In the name of the almighty God I ask you to make me wise in my decisions and not to be careless, by the power and merit of King Solomon this will be done.

You angel Ithuriel I bind you to this seal in the name of King Solomon your master so that my enthusiasm will remain high for the things I know I must do and for those things I want to do… Help me now!

8.   Sit in silence and just feel the power of God coursing through you. Visualize the power coming though the top of your head and out of your hands into the talisman. Watch it glow.

9.   Place the Talisman down and say "Go you angels of this mighty seal, go and fulfill my request and guide me in the name of the great king Solomon who binds you. Amen

10.   Leave the talisman on the Altar until the candle and incense are extinguished.

11.   When the candles and Incense have burned down, you are free to use the talisman how you please; you can wear it, put in your pocket or whatever is most appropriate for you based on the purpose of the talisman.

Ritual 16 – To Achieve Healing of a Certain Part of the Body

The Second Pentacle of Mars

Ritual should be done On a Tuesday

1. Setup the Altar as such: The Talisman will always be in the middle. On the right side, place the candle/s. On the left Place the Incense.

2. Charge the Talisman

3. Light the Blue candle

4. Light the incense

5.   Pick up the talisman and place it your hands (Either hand or both)

6.   Now sit in front of your altar and think about the area of your body you wish to be health. Once you have built a sufficient feeling and image of what it is you want.

7.   Recite the following verse with Conviction "In Him was life, and the life was the light of man."

8.   Sit in silence and just feel the power of God coursing through you. Visualize the power coming though the top of your head and out of your hands into the talisman. Watch it glow.

9.   Place the Talisman down and say "In gratitude I come before you YHVH-Elohim of the universe, I know that you will grant this wish for me through this holy Talisman of Solomon Your servant.

10.   Leave the talisman on the Altar until the candle and incense are extinguished.

11.   When the candles and Incense have burned down, you are free to use the talisman how you please; you can wear it, put in your pocket or whatever is most appropriate for you based on the purpose of the talisman. (In this instance place it on the body part you need healing in).

Ritual 17 – To Protect You From The Ill Intent of Other
The Third Pentacle of Mars

Ritual should be done On a Tuesday

1. Setup the Altar as such: The Talisman will always be in the middle. On the right side, place the candle/s. On the left Place the Incense.

2. Charge the Talisman

3. Light the Black candle

4. Light the incense

5.   Pick up the talisman and place it your hands (Either hand or both)

6.   Now sit in front of your altar and think about the person or persons that you want to be protected from. Perhaps they are trying to sabotage you or have ill intent. Once you have built a sufficient feeling and image of what it is you want.

7.   Recite the following verse with Conviction "Who is so great a God as our God?"

8.   Invoke the Names of God:

Oh Mighty El-Shaddai - Eloha, the one who has no boundary, I ask you to protect me from the evil intents of man. Do so by the merit of your servant King Solomon.

9.   Sit in silence and just feel the power of God coursing through you. Visualize the power coming though the top of your head and out of your hands into the talisman. Watch it glow.

10.   Place the Talisman down and say "In gratitude I come before you El-Shaddai - Eloha of the universe, I know that you will grant this wish for me through this holy Talisman of Solomon Your servant.

11.   Leave the talisman on the Altar until the candle and incense are extinguished.

12.   When the candles and Incense have burned down, you are free to use the talisman how you please; you can wear it, put in your pocket or whatever is most appropriate for you based on the purpose of the talisman.

Ritual 18 – To Conqueror Your Enemy
The Fourth Pentacle of Mars

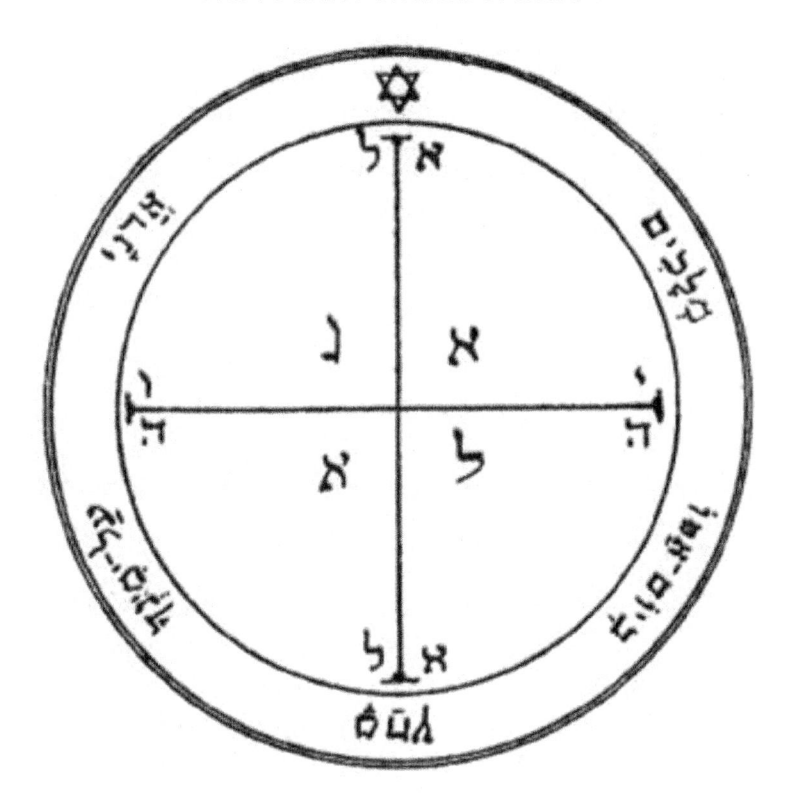

Ritual should be done On a Tuesday

1. Setup the Altar as such: The Talisman will always be in the middle. On the right side, place the candle/s. On the left Place the Incense.

2. Charge the Talisman

3. Light the Red candle

4. Light the incense

5. Pick up the talisman and place it your hands (Either hand or both)

6. Now sit in front of your altar and think about the person or persons that you want to defeat .Once you have built a sufficient feeling and image of what it is you want.

7. Recite the following verse with Conviction "The Lord at thy right hand shall wound even Kings in the day of His Wrath."

8. Invoke the Names of God:

Oh Mighty Agla – Adonai-El, the one who has no boundary, I ask you to give me victory over my enemies that they may tremble before me. Do so by the merit of your servant King Solomon.

9. Sit in silence and just feel the power of God coursing through you. Visualize the power coming though the top of your head and out of your hands into the talisman. Watch it glow.

10. Place the Talisman down and say "In gratitude I come before you Agla – Adonai-El, of the universe, I know that you will grant this wish for me through this holy Talisman of Solomon Your servant.

11. Leave the talisman on the Altar until the candle and incense are extinguished.

12. When the candles and Incense have burned down, you are free to use the talisman how you please; you can wear it, put in your pocket or whatever is most appropriate for you based on the purpose of the talisman.

Ritual 19 – To Gain Control Over Demons or Other Spiritual Entities

The Fifth Pentacle of Mars

Ritual should be done On a Tuesday

1. Setup the Altar as such: The Talisman will always be in the middle. On the right side, place the candle/s. On the left Place the Incense.

2. Charge the Talisman

3. Light the Black candle

4. Light the incense

5. Pick up the talisman and place it your hands (Either hand or both)

6. Now sit in front of your altar and think about the desire to gain the ability to control any spirit you wish. (You can use this Talisman as a tool in your other rituals) .Once you have built a sufficient feeling and image of what it is you want.

7. Recite the following verse with Conviction "Thou shalt go upon the lion and added, the young lion and the dragon shalt thou tread under thy feet."

8. Sit in silence and just feel the power of God coursing through you. Visualize the power coming though the top of your head and out of your hands into the talisman. Watch it glow.

9. Place the Talisman down and say "In gratitude I come before you King of the universe, I know that you will grant this wish for me through this holy Talisman of Solomon Your servant.

10. Leave the talisman on the Altar until the candle and incense are extinguished.

11. When the candles and Incense have burned down, you are free to use the talisman how you please; you can wear it, put in your pocket or whatever is most appropriate for you based on the purpose of the talisman.

Ritual 20 – To Prevent Harm from Others
The Sixth Pentacle of Mars

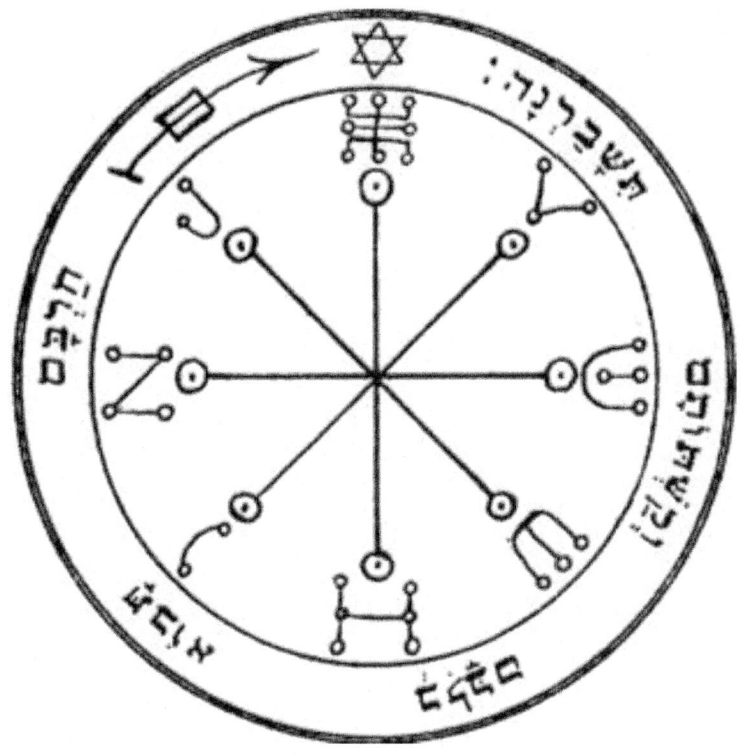

Ritual should be done On a Tuesday

1. Setup the Altar as such: The Talisman will always be in the middle. On the right side, place the candle/s. On the left Place the Incense.

2. Charge the Talisman

3. Light the Black Candle

4. Light the incense

5. Pick up the talisman and place it your hands (Either hand or both)

6. Now sit in front of your altar and think about the person or persons that you want to be protected from. Perhaps they are trying to sabotage you or want to harm you. Once you have built a sufficient feeling and image of what it is you want.

7. Recite the following verse with Conviction "Their sword shall enter into their own heart, and their bow shall be broken."

8. Sit in silence and just feel the power of God coursing through you. Visualize the power coming though the top of your head and out of your hands into the talisman. Watch it glow.

9. Place the Talisman down and say "In gratitude I come before you YHVH the great protector of the universe, I know that you will grant this wish for me through this holy Talisman of Solomon Your servant.

10. Leave the talisman on the Altar until the candle and incense are extinguished.

11. When the candles and Incense have burned down, you are free to use the talisman how you please; you can wear it, put in your pocket or whatever is most appropriate for you based on the purpose of the talisman.

Ritual 21 – To Control the Weather
The Seventh Pentacle of Mars

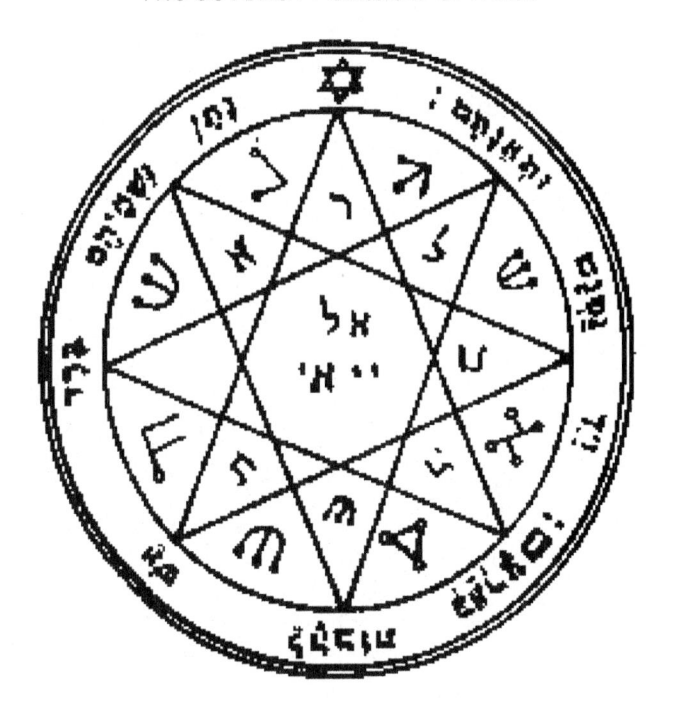

Ritual should be done On a Tuesday

1. Setup the Altar as such: The Talisman will always be in the middle. On the right side, place the candle/s. On the left Place the Incense.

2. Charge the Talisman

3. Light the Red AND Black Candles

4. Light the incense

5. Pick up the talisman and place it your hands (Either hand or both)

6. Now sit in front of your altar and think about the desire to control the weather, it can be anywhere in the world. Once you have built a sufficient feeling and image of what it is you want.

7. Recite the following verse with Conviction "He gave them hail for rain, and flaming fire in their land. He smote their vines also, and their fig-trees."

Invoke the names of God: Oh Mighty EL- Yee-Ya the controller of the tempests, I ask you to give me control over earth, fire, water and Air. Do so by the merit of your servant King Solomon.

8. Sit in silence and just feel the power of God coursing through you. Visualize the power coming though the top of your head and out of your hands into the talisman. Watch it glow.

9. Place the Talisman down and say "In gratitude I come before you EL- Yee-Ya the great controller of the tempests, I know that you will grant this wish for me through this holy Talisman of Solomon Your servant.

10. Leave the talisman on the Altar until the candle and incense are extinguished.

11. When the candles and Incense have burned down, you are free to use the talisman how you please; you can wear it, put in your pocket or whatever is most appropriate for you based on the purpose of the talisman.

Ritual 22 – To Gain Control Over Any Sentient Being
The First Pentacle of the Sun

Ritual should be done On a Sunday

1.	Setup the Altar as such: The Talisman will always be in the middle. On the right side, place the candle/s. On the left Place the Incense.

2.	Charge the Talisman

3.	Light the Orange Candle

4.	Light the incense

5.	Pick up the talisman and place it your hands (Either hand or both)

6. Now sit in front of your altar and think about the desire to control others be it humans or animals or what have you, think about the reason why. Once you have built a sufficient feeling and image of what it is you want.

7. Recite the following verse with Conviction "Behold His face and form by whom all things were made, and Whom all creatures obey."

Invoke the names of God: Oh Mighty EL- Shaddai the most powerful God, I ask you to give me control over _____. Do so by the merit of your servant King Solomon.

8. Sit in silence and just feel the power of God coursing through you. Visualize the power coming though the top of your head and out of your hands into the talisman. Watch it glow.

9. Place the Talisman down and say "In gratitude I come before you EL- Shaddai the great controller of the man and beast, I know that you will grant this wish for me through this holy Talisman of Solomon Your servant.

10. Leave the talisman on the Altar until the candle and incense are extinguished.

11. When the candles and Incense have burned down, you are free to use the talisman how you please; you can wear it, put in your pocket or whatever is most appropriate for you based on the purpose of the talisman.

Ritual 23 – To Humble Someone
The Second Pentacle of the Sun

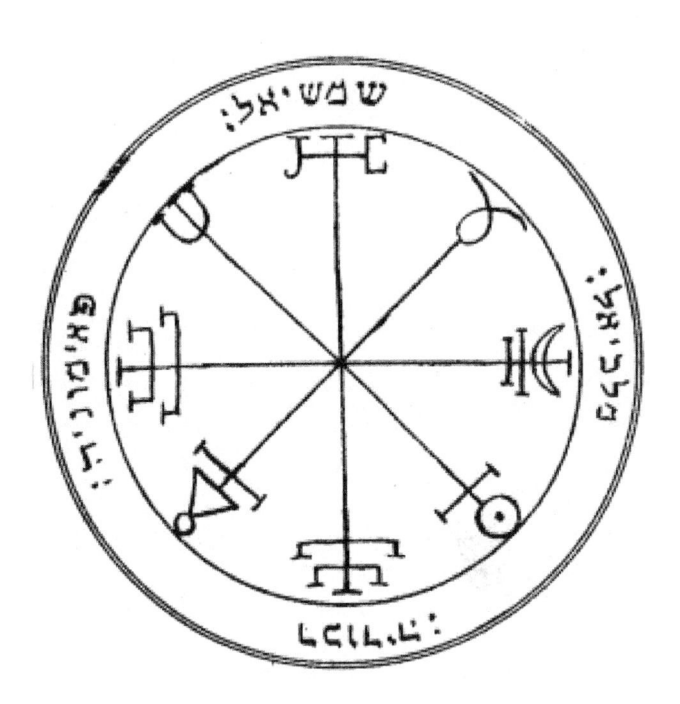

Ritual should be done On a Sunday

1. Setup the Altar as such: The Talisman will always be in the middle. On the right side, place the candle/s. On the left Place the Incense.

2. Charge the Talisman

3. Light the Orange candle

4. Light the incense

5.   Pick up the talisman and place it your hands (Either hand or both)

6.   Now sit in front of your altar and think about the person you want to humble. Why do you want to humble them? Do they deserve to be taken down a notch? Once you have built a sufficient feeling and image of what it is you want.

7.   Now Invoke the angels:

Oh Benevolent angel Shemeshiel I ask and command you in the name of King Solomon your lord that you give me the power to humble_____. By this great seal shall it be so.

To you angel Paimoniah I ask and command you in the name of King Solomon your lord that you Humble _____. In the name of King Solomon make this so.

You the Great Angel Rekhodiah, In the name of the almighty God I ask you you to subjugate and place _____ under my control so they may be humbled, by the power and merit of King Solomon this will be done.

You angel Melkhiel I bind you to this seal in the name of King Solomon your master so that my magickal abilities will remain high so I can have the ability to subjugate and control others. Help me now!

8.   Sit in silence and just feel the power of God coursing through you. Visualize the power coming though the top of your head and out of your hands into the talisman. Watch it glow.

9.   Place the Talisman down and say "Go you angels of this mighty seal, go and fulfill my request and guide me in the name of the great king Solomon who binds you. Amen

10.   Leave the talisman on the Altar until the candle and incense are extinguished.

11.   When the candles and Incense have burned down, you are free to use the talisman how you please; you can wear it, put in your pocket or whatever is most appropriate for you based on the purpose of the talisman.

Ritual 24 – To Increase Your Wealth Significantly
The Third Pentacle of the Sun

Ritual should be done On a Sunday

1. Setup the Altar as such: The Talisman will always be in the middle. On the right side, place the candle/s. On the left Place the Incense.

2. Charge the Talisman

3. Light the Orange Candle

4.   Light the incense

5.   Pick up the talisman and place it your hands (Either hand or both)

6.   Now sit in front of your altar and think about the desire to control others be it humans or animals or what have you, think about the reason why. Once you have built a sufficient feeling and image of what it is you want.

7.   Recite the following verse with Conviction "My Kingdom is an everlasting Kingdom, and my dominion endures from age to age."

Invoke the names of God: Oh Mighty YHVH the most powerful name, I ask you to give me unlimited wealth, more than I will ever need. Do so by the merit of your servant King Solomon.

8.   Sit in silence and just feel the power of God coursing through you. Visualize the power coming though the top of your head and out of your hands into the talisman. Watch it glow.

9.   Place the Talisman down and say "In gratitude I come before you YHVH the great provider. I know that you will grant this wish for me through this holy Talisman of Solomon Your servant.

10.   Leave the talisman on the Altar until the candle and incense are extinguished.

11.   When the candles and Incense have burned down, you are free to use the talisman how you please; you can wear it, put in your pocket or whatever is most appropriate for you based on the purpose of the talisman

tual 25 – To Help You See Spirits Wherever They May Be

The Fourth Pentacle of the Sun

Ritual should be done On a Sunday

1. Setup the Altar as such: The Talisman will always be in the middle. On the right side, place the candle/s. On the left Place the Incense.

2.	Charge the Talisman

3.	Light the Orange Candle

4.	Light the incense

5.	Pick up the talisman and place it your hands (Either hand or both)

6.	Now sit in front of your altar and think about the desire to see the spirits that inhabit the earth. This will help you see spirits wherever they may be. Once you have built a sufficient feeling and image of what it is you want.

7.	Recite the following verse with Conviction "Lighten mine eyes that I sleep not in death, lest mine enemy say, I have prevailed against him."

Invoke the names of God: Oh Most Powerful YHVH-Adonai the king of all that is seen and unseen, I ask you to give me unlimited spiritual sight that I may see the spirits that abound. Do so by the merit of your servant King Solomon.

8.	Sit in silence and just feel the power of God coursing through you. Visualize the power coming though the top of your head and out of your hands into the talisman. Watch it glow.

9.	Place the Talisman down and say "In gratitude I come before you YHVH- Adonai the great provider. I know that you will grant this wish for me through this holy Talisman of Solomon Your servant.

10.	Leave the talisman on the Altar until the candle and incense are extinguished.

11.	When the candles and Incense have burned down, you are free to use the talisman how you please; you can wear it, put in your pocket or whatever is most appropriate for you based on the purpose of the talisman

Ritual 26 – To Traverse Great Distances In Short Periods of Time
The Fifth Pentacle of the Sun

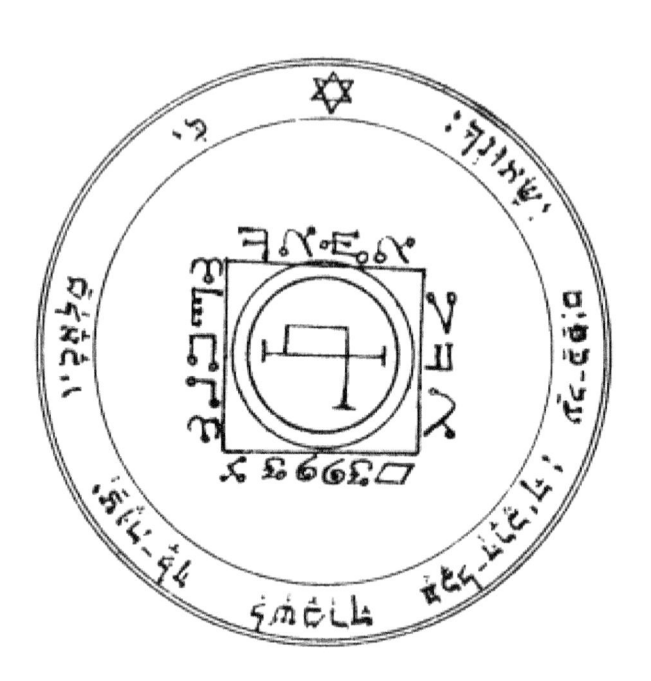

Ritual should be done On a Sunday

1. Setup the Altar as such: The Talisman will always be in the middle. On the right side, place the candle/s. On the left Place the Incense.

2. Charge the Talisman

3. Light the Orange Candle

4. Light the incense

5. Pick up the talisman and place it your hands (Either hand or both)

6. Now sit in front of your altar and think about the long distance you must travel and how you would like to be able to traverse it in a short period of time . Once you have built a sufficient feeling and image of what it is you want.

7. Recite the following verse with Conviction "He shall give His Angels charge over thee, to keep thee in all thy ways. They shall bear thee up in their hands."

8. Sit in silence and just feel the power of God coursing through you. Visualize the power coming though the top of your head and out of your hands into the talisman. Watch it glow.

9. Place the Talisman down and say " May My travels be safe and Swift so mote it be"

10. Leave the talisman on the Altar until the candle and incense are extinguished.

11. When the candles and Incense have burned down, you are free to use the talisman how you please; you can wear it, put in your pocket or whatever is most appropriate for you based on the purpose of the Talisman.

Ritual 27 – To Confer Upon Oneself Visibility
The Sixth Pentacle of the Sun

This Talisman has been used to confer invisibility. I am not sure it works in the way that one might think. I feel this is a talisman that will make you go unnoticed especially for you do not want to be noticed in a crowd or at an event. If you want to avoid a certain person or people, this is the talisman I feel will work for you.

Ritual should be done On a Sunday

1. Setup the Altar as such: The Talisman will always be in the middle. On the right side, place the candle/s. On the left Place the Incense.

2. Charge the Talisman

3. Light the Orange Candle

4. Light the incense

5. Pick up the talisman and place it your hands (Either hand or both)

6. Now sit in front of your altar and think about the need to be invisible in the various ways that this word can be used. Once you have built a sufficient feeling and image of what it is you want.

7. Recite the following verse with Conviction "Let their eyes be darkened that they see not; and make their loins continually to shake. They have eyes and see not."

8. Sit in silence and just feel the power of God coursing through you. Visualize the power coming though the top of your head and out of your hands into the talisman. Watch it glow.

9. Place the Talisman down and say "May I disappear to the sight of man and beast. So Mote it Be"

10. Leave the talisman on the Altar until the candle and incense are extinguished.

11. When the candles and Incense have burned down, you are free to use the talisman how you please; you can wear it, put in your pocket or whatever is most appropriate for you based on the purpose of the Talisman.

Ritual 28 – To Get Unstuck
The Seventh Pentacle of the Sun

Ritual should be done On a Sunday

1. Setup the Altar as such: The Talisman will always be in the middle. On the right side, place the candle/s. On the left Place the Incense.

2. Charge the Talisman

3.	Light the Orange candle

4.	Light the incense

5.	Pick up the talisman and place it your hands (Either hand or both)

6.	Now sit in front of your altar and think of your need to get unstuck in life in general or from a specific situation or relationship. Once you have built a sufficient feeling and image of what it is you want.

7.	Recite the following verse with Conviction "Thou hast broken my bonds in sunder. I will offer unto thee the sacrifice of thanksgiving, and will call upon the Name of Jehovah."

8.	Now Invoke the order of angels and the 6 angels within the seal:

You the order of Seraphim, I bind you to this seal in the name of King Solomon your master that you burn away my current obstacles so I may be free.

You the order of Kerubim, you of the great and powerful order, you who protect those who call upon you, guide me that I will not enter into stagnation either body, mind and spirit.

Oh great angel Ariel, The lion of God protect me in all my ways so I may take the risks I need to take to bring my life to fruition. In the name of your King Solomon I bind you to this seal of protection.

In the name of the almighty and your master King Solomon, angel Tharsis I bind you to this Seal so that you may be my guide when I find myself in an unknown situation. Make my decisions wise and clear. I bind you to this seal, so mote it be.

Oh you Angels of the elements Chasan, Arel, Phorlakh and Taliahad help me so I may be set free of my current obstacles. In the name of the Great King Solomon your lord.

9. Sit in silence and just feel the power of God coursing through you. Visualize the power coming though the top of your head and out of your hands into the talisman. Watch it glow.

10. Place the Talisman down and say "Go you of the great angelic orders, go and do my bidding and unbind me in the name of the great King Solomon. Amen

11. Leave the talisman on the Altar until the candle and incense are extinguished.

12. When the candles and Incense have burned down, you are free to use the talisman how you please; you can wear it, put in your pocket or whatever is most appropriate for you based on the purpose of the talisman.

Ritual 29 – To Gain friend and Or Lover
The First Pentacle of Venus

Ritual should be done On a Friday

1. Setup the Altar as such: The Talisman will always be in the middle. On the right side, place the candle/s. On the left Place the Incense.

2. Charge the Talisman

Light the Pink and OR red candles

4. Light the incense

5. Pick up the talisman and place it your hands (Either hand or both)

6. Now sit in front of your altar and think about the need to either make more friends or to find a lover. Once you have built a sufficient feeling and image of what it is you want.

7. Now Invoke the angels:

Oh Benevolent angel Nogahiel I ask and command you in the name of King Solomon your lord that you give me the power and ability to make friends (OR) to secure the love of _____ By this great seal shall it be so.

To you angel Acheliah I ask and command you in the name of King Solomon your lord that you bring _____ to me (Or) to enhance my personal magnetism so as to attract the attention of those I wish to know. In the name of King Solomon make this so.

You the Great Angel Socodiah, In the name of the almighty God I ask you to give me the courage to be more interactive with my fellow man...By the power and merit of King Solomon this will be done.

You angel Nangariel I bind you to this seal in the name of King Solomon your master so that my magickal abilities will remain high so I can gain the love and admiration of others. Help me now!

8. Sit in silence and just feel the power of God coursing through you. Visualize the power coming though the top of your head and out of your hands into the talisman. Watch it glow.

9. Place the Talisman down and say "Go you angels of this mighty seal, go and fulfill my request and guide me in the name of the great king Solomon who binds you. Amen

10. Leave the talisman on the Altar until the candle and incense are extinguished.

11. When the candles and Incense have burned down, you are free to use the talisman how you please; you can wear it, put in your pocket or whatever is most appropriate for you based on the purpose of the talisman.

Ritual 30 – To Obtain Grace and Honor
The Second Pentacle of Venus

Ritual should be done On a Friday

1. Setup the Altar as such: The Talisman will always be in the middle. On the right side, place the candle/s. On the left Place the Incense.

2. Charge the Talisman

3. Light the Pink OR Red Candle

4. Light the incense

5. Pick up the talisman and place it your hands (Either hand or both)

6.　Now sit in front of your altar and think about the need to be obtain grace and honor, it could be a general request or for a specific occasion. Once you have built a sufficient feeling and image of what it is you want.

7.　Recite the following verse with Conviction "Place me as a signet upon thine heart, as a signet upon thine arm, for love is strong as death."

8.　Sit in silence and just feel the power of God coursing through you. Visualize the power coming though the top of your head and out of your hands into the talisman. Watch it glow.

9.　Place the Talisman down and say "I Have Grace and Honor. So Mote it Be"

10.　Leave the talisman on the Altar until the candle and incense are extinguished.

11.　When the candles and Incense have burned down, you are free to use the talisman how you please; you can wear it, put in your pocket or whatever is most appropriate for you based on the purpose of the Talisman.

Ritual 31 – Talisman of Love and Attraction
The Third Pentacle of Venus

This Talisman is supposedly so powerful that if you just show it to the person you want; they will be attracted to you and want to be with you.

Ritual should be done On a Friday

1.	Setup the Altar as such: The Talisman will always be in the middle. On the right side, place the candle/s. On the left Place the Incense.

2.	Charge the Talisman

3.	Light the Red OR Pink Candles

4.	Light the incense

5.	Pick up the talisman and place it your hands (Either hand or both)

6.	Now sit in front of your altar and think about the person or persons you want to attract, think about them clearly. Once you have built a sufficient feeling and image of what it is you want.

7.	Recite the following verse with Conviction "And the Elohim blessed them, and the Elohim said unto them, 'Be ye fruitful, and multiply, and replenish the earth, and subdue it."

8.	Invoke the names of God: Oh Mighty YHVH-Adonai the most powerful of names, I ask you to give me unlimited personal Magnetism, more than I will ever need. Do so by the merit of your servant King Solomon.

9.	Invoke the Angels (Since there is not much known about these angels I will use a generic invocation)

"Oh Mighty angels Ruach, Achides, Aegalmiel, Monachiel, Degaliel by the powers vested in this great seal of King Solomon I bind you and command you to make _____ be irresistibly attracted to me. It will be done so mote it be"

10. Sit in silence and just feel the power of God coursing through you. Visualize the power coming though the top of your head and out of your hands into the talisman. Watch it glow.

11. Place the Talisman down and say "In gratitude I come before you YHVH-Adonai the great provider. I know that you will grant this wish for me through this holy Talisman of Solomon Your servant.

12. Leave the talisman on the Altar until the candle and incense are extinguished.

13. When the candles and Incense have burned down, you are free to use the talisman how you please; you can wear it, put in your pocket or whatever is most appropriate for you based on the purpose of the talisman.

Ritual 32 – Talisman to Attract a Specific Person
The Fourth Pentacle of Venus

Ritual should be done On a Friday

1. Setup the Altar as such: The Talisman will always be in the middle. On the right side, place the candle/s. On the left Place the Incense.

2. Charge the Talisman

3. Light the Red OR Pink Candles

4. Light the incense

5. Pick up the talisman and place it your hands (Either hand or both)

6. Now sit in front of your altar and think about the person you want to attract, think about them clearly. Once you have built a sufficient feeling and image of what it is you want.

7. Recite the following verse with Conviction "This is bone of my bones, and flesh of my flesh. And they two were one flesh."

8. Invoke the names of God: Oh Mighty YHVH- the you who can soften and harden every persons heart, I ask you to send _____ my way and have them be irresistibly attracted to me. Do so by the merit of your servant King Solomon.

9. Sit in silence and just feel the power of God coursing through you. Visualize the power coming though the top of your head and out of your hands into the talisman. Watch it glow.

10. Place the Talisman down and say "In gratitude I come before you YHVH the Keeper of hearts. I know that you will grant this wish for me through this holy Talisman of Solomon Your servant.

11. Leave the talisman on the Altar until the candle and incense are extinguished.

12. When the candles and Incense have burned down, you are free to use the talisman how you please; you can wear it, put in your pocket or whatever is most appropriate for you based on the purpose of the talisman.

Ritual 33 – Talisman to Attract a Specific Person by Showing them the Talisman

The Fifth Pentacle of Venus

Used to cause love and attraction in another person upon showing it to them, very similar to a previous talisman.

Ritual should be done On a Friday

1.	Setup the Altar as such: The Talisman will always be in the middle. On the right side, place the candle/s. On the left Place the Incense.

2.	Charge the Talisman

3.	Light the Red OR Pink Candles

4.	Light the incense

5.	Pick up the talisman and place it your hands (Either hand or both)

6.	Now sit in front of your altar and think about the person you want to attract, think about them clearly. Once you have built a sufficient feeling and image of what it is you want.

7.	Recite the following verse with Conviction "My heart is like wax; it is melted in the midst of my bowels."

8.	Sit in silence and just feel the power of God coursing through you. Visualize the power coming though the top of your head and out of your hands into the talisman. Watch it glow.

9.	Place the Talisman down and say "_____ Will be attracted to me , they will be bound by this seal. So it shall be done.

10.	Leave the talisman on the Altar until the candle and incense are extinguished.

11.	When the candles and Incense have burned down, you are free to use the talisman how you please; you can wear it, put in your pocket or whatever is most appropriate for you based on the purpose of the talisman.

Ritual 34 – Talisman to Increase Your Personal Magnetism
The First Pentacle of Mercury

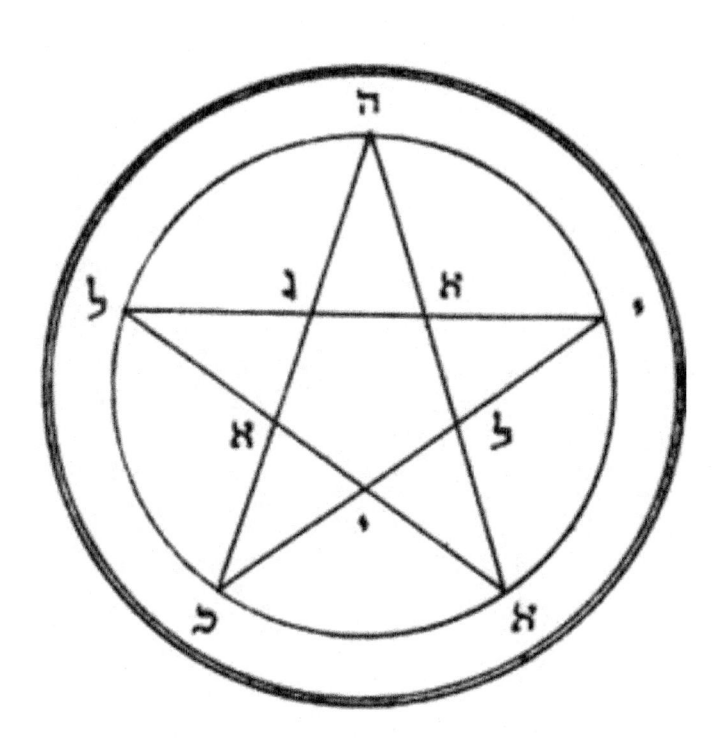

Ritual should be done On a Wednesday

1. Setup the Altar as such: The Talisman will always be in the middle. On the right side, place the candle/s. On the left Place the Incense.

2. Charge the Talisman

3. Light the Yellow Candle

4. Light the incense

5. Pick up the talisman and place it your hands (Either hand or both)

6. Now sit in front of your altar and think about your desire to enhance your personal magnetism. Once you have built a sufficient feeling and image of what it is you want.

7. Invoke the Angels:

Oh great and mighty Angel Yekahel Make me irresistible to the people I encounter, by the power of this great seal of King Solomon your lord, I implore you to do so.

You Angel Agiel by the power vested in this magickal seal of your Lord King Solomon, I command that you not only make me irresistible to the people I encounter but also to make me mentally strong so I may appreciate my power So Mote it be.

8. Sit in silence and just feel the power of God coursing through you. Visualize the power coming though the top of your head and out of your hands into the talisman. Watch it glow.

9. Place the Talisman down and say "In gratitude I thank you oh mighty angels. I know that you will grant this wish for me through this holy Talisman of Solomon Your servant.

10.   Leave the talisman on the Altar until the candle and incense are extinguished.

11.   When the candles and Incense have burned down, you are free to use the talisman how you please; you can wear it, put in your pocket or whatever is most appropriate for you based on the purpose of the talisman.

Ritual 35 – Talisman to Help you When all Seems Lost.
The Second Pentacle of Mercury

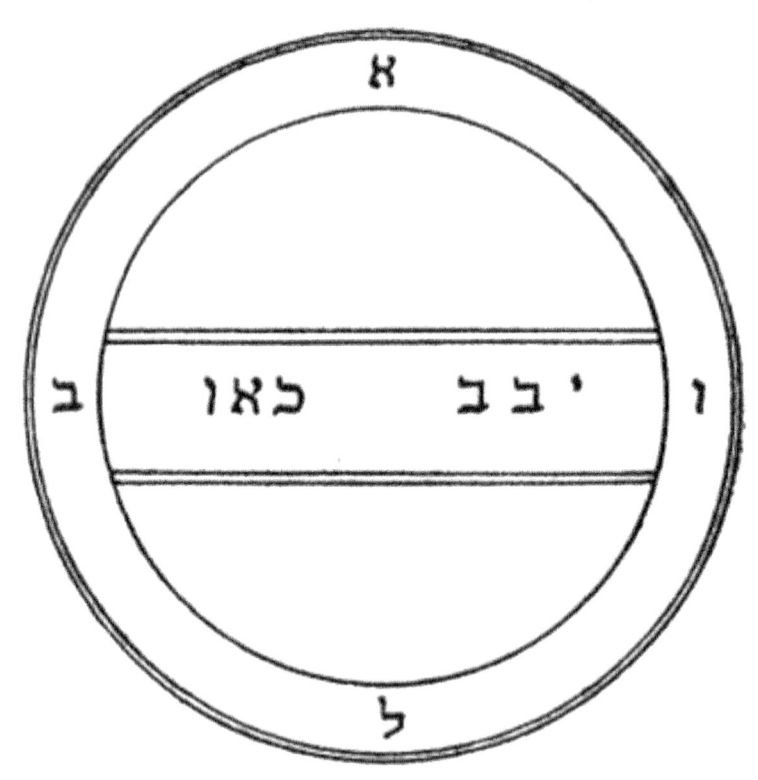

Ritual should be done On a Wednesday

1. Setup the Altar as such: The Talisman will always be in the middle. On the right side, place the candle/s. On the left Place the Incense.

2. Charge the Talisman

3. Light the Yellow Candle

4. Light the incense

5. Pick up the talisman and place it your hands (Either hand or both)

6. Now sit in front of your altar and think about your situation that you believe is impossible to solve. Once you have built a sufficient feeling and image of what it is you want.

7. Invoke the Angels:

Oh great and mighty Angel Boel , you who commands the four corners of the earth by the power of this great seal of King Solomon your lord, I implore you to help me remedy this pressing issue. You will do so. Amen

8. Sit in silence and just feel the power of God coursing through you. Visualize the power coming though the top of your head and out of your hands into the talisman. Watch it glow.

9. Place the Talisman down and say "In gratitude I thank you Boel, I know that you will grant this wish for me through this holy Talisman of Solomon Your servant.

10. Leave the talisman on the Altar until the candle and incense are extinguished.

11. When the candles and Incense have burned down, you are free to use the talisman how you please; you can wear it, put in your pocket or whatever is most appropriate for you based on the purpose of the talisman

itual 36 – Talisman to Help you Increase your Writing and Literary Skills

The Third Pentacle of Mercury

Ritual should be done On a Wednesday

1. Setup the Altar as such: The Talisman will always be in the middle. On the right side, place the candle/s. On the left Place the Incense.

2. Charge the Talisman

3. Light the Yellow Candle

4. Light the incense

5. Pick up the talisman and place it your hands (Either hand or both)

6. Now sit in front of your altar and think about your desire to enhance your writing and literary skills, see yourself writing with ease. Once you have built a sufficient feeling and image of what it is you want.

7. Now Invoke the angels:

Oh wise angel Kokaviel I ask and command you in the name of King Solomon your lord that you give me the mental capacity and power to learn and to write with ease all that I choose to write on. Be my Muse. By this great seal shall it be so.

To you angel Gheoriah I ask and command you in the name of King Solomon your lord that you open my mind and spirit to the great mysteries of creativity. We all have creation in our souls, help me discover it. In the name of King Solomon make this so.

You the Great Angel Savaniah, I ask and command you in the name of King Solomon your lord that you open my mind and spirit to the great mysteries of creativity.. In the name of King Solomon you will make this so for you are bound to me.

You angel Hokmahiel I bind you to this seal in the name of King Solomon your master so that my ability to write and create will remain high so I can gain the love and admiration of others through my work. Help me now!

8. Sit in silence and just feel the power of God coursing through you. Visualize the power coming though the top of your head and out of your hands into the talisman. Watch it glow.

9. Place the Talisman down and say "Go you angels of this mighty seal, go and fulfill my request and guide me in the name of the great king Solomon who binds you. Amen

10. Leave the talisman on the Altar until the candle and incense are extinguished.

11. When the candles and Incense have burned down, you are free to use the talisman how you please; you can wear it, put in your pocket or whatever is most appropriate for you based on the purpose of the talisman.

Ritual 37 – Talisman to Help you Gain Knowledge and Understanding on Any Topic You Desire.
The Fourth Pentacle of Mercury

Ritual should be done On a Wednesday

1. Setup the Altar as such: The Talisman will always be in the middle. On the right side, place the candle/s. On the left Place the Incense.

2. Charge the Talisman

3. Light the Yellow Candle

4. Light the incense

5. Pick up the talisman and place it your hands (Either hand or both)

6. Now sit in front of your altar and think about the topic you want to learn, it can be more than one. Once you have built a sufficient feeling and image of what it is you want.

7. Recite the following verse with Conviction "Wisdom and virtue are in his house, and the Knowledge of all things remains with him forever." "God, fix Thou the Volatile, and let there be unto the void restriction."

8. Invoke the Name of God: EL the mighty God of creation, he who has brought forth knowledge of all kinds. Bless me by the merits of this great seal of your servant King Solomon with the knowledge and wisdom I require.

9. Sit in silence and just feel the power of God coursing through you. Visualize the power coming though the top of your head and out of your hands into the talisman. Watch it glow.

10. Place the Talisman down and say "Thank you El, for you are the granter of all knowledge.

11. Leave the talisman on the Altar until the candle and incense are extinguished.

12. When the candles and Incense have burned down, you are free to use the talisman how you please; you can wear it, put in your pocket or whatever is most appropriate for you based on the purpose of the talisman.

Ritual 38 – Talisman to Help you Open and Doors and Portals

The Fifth Pentacle of Mercury

Serves to open doors and portals of any kind, be it spiritual or physical, no barrier is too great for its power. .

Ritual should be done On a Wednesday

1. Setup the Altar as such: The Talisman will always be in the middle. On the right side, place the candle/s. On the left Place the Incense.

2. Charge the Talisman

3. Light the Yellow Candle

4. Light the incense

5. Pick up the talisman and place it your hands (Either hand or both)

6. Now sit in front of your altar and think about the spiritual portal you wish to enter. Once you have built a sufficient feeling and image of what it is you want.

7. Recite the following verse with Conviction "Lift up your heads, O ye gates, and be ye lift up ye everlasting doors, and the King of Glory shall come in."

8. Invoke the Name of God: YHVH-EL the mighty God of creation and father of us all, he who has no barrier. Bless me by the merits of this great seal of your servant King Solomon with the ability to open and enter spiritual portals that have been closed to those who are uninitiated. This will be done.

9. Sit in silence and just feel the power of God coursing through you. Visualize the power coming though the top of your head and out of your hands into the talisman. Watch it glow.

10. Place the Talisman down and say "Thank you YHVH-EL, our father, for you are the Guardian of all knowledge and dimensions.

11. Leave the talisman on the Altar until the candle and incense are extinguished.

12. When the candles and Incense have burned down, you are free to use the talisman how you please; you can wear it, put in your pocket or whatever is most appropriate for you based on the purpose of the talisman.

Ritual 39 – Talisman to Help You To Help You Gain Access To Secret Knowledge.

The First Pentacle of the Moon

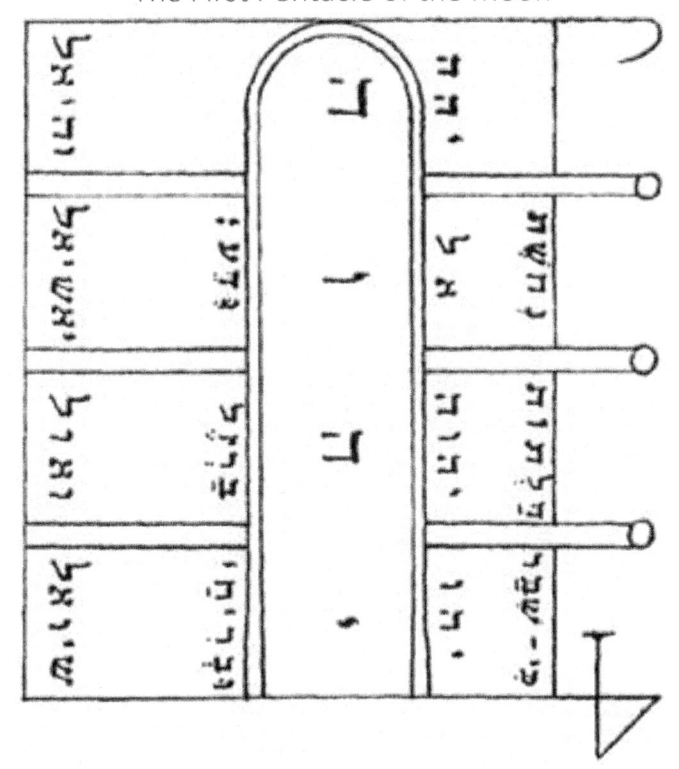

Ritual should be done On a Monday

1. Setup the Altar as such: The Talisman will always be in the middle. On the right side, place the candle/s. On the left Place the Incense.

2. Charge the Talisman

3. Light the Silver Candle

4. Light the incense

Pick up the talisman and place it your hands (Either hand or both)

6. Now sit in front of your altar and think about your desire to learn hidden and esoteric wisdom. What do you want to learn? Once you have built a sufficient feeling and image of what it is you want.

7. Now say the following verse with conviction: "He hath broken the Gates of brass, and smitten the bars of iron in sunder."

13. Now Invoke the Name of God: YHVH-AL the mighty God of hidden wisdom. Bless me by the merits of this great seal of your servant King Solomon with the ability to learn the great secret mysteries. May it be your will Amen.

8. Now Invoke the angels:

Oh wise angel Schioel I ask and command you in the name of King Solomon your lord that you give me the mental capacity and power to learn the great mysteries of the universe. Be my Guide. By this great seal shall it be so.

To you angel Vaol I ask and command you in the name of King Solomon your lord that you open my mind and spirit to the great mysteries of creativity that will help me understand the mysteries of the deep. In the name of King Solomon make this so.

You the Great Angel Yashiel, I ask and command you in the name of King Solomon your lord that you open my mind and spirit to Heavens wisdom and bounty. In the name of King Solomon you will make this so for you are bound to me.

You angel Vehiel I bind you to this seal in the name of King Solomon your master to help me raise my mind and spirit to the spiritual dimensions in which the great mysteries can be found. So Mote it be.

9. Sit in silence and just feel the power of God coursing through you. Visualize the power coming though the top of your head and out of your hands into the talisman. Watch it glow.

10. Place the Talisman down and say "Go you angels of this mighty seal, go and fulfill my request and guide me in the name of the great king Solomon who binds you. Amen

11. Leave the talisman on the Altar until the candle and incense are extinguished.

12. When the candles and Incense have burned down, you are free to use the talisman how you please; you can wear it, put in your pocket or whatever is most appropriate for you based on the purpose of the talisman.

Ritual 40 – Talisman to Protect You From Natural Disasters
The Second Pentacle of the Moon

Ritual should be done On a Monday

1   Setup the Altar as such: The Talisman will always be in the middle. On the right side, place the candle/s. On the left Place the Incense.

2   Charge the Talisman

3   Light the Silver Candle

4   Light the incense

5   Pick up the talisman and place it your hands (Either hand or both)

6   Now sit in front of your altar and think about your desire to be protected during natural disasters, this is good especially if you live in a region prone to them. Once you have built a sufficient feeling and image of what it is you want.

7   Now say the following verse with conviction: "In Elohim have I put my trust, I will not fear, what can man do unto me?"

8   Now Invoke the Name of God: EL the mighty God and protector. Bless me by the merits of this great seal of your servant King Solomon with safety and security when nature unleashes her wrath. May it be your will .

9   Now Invoke the angel/s:

Oh protector angel Abariel I ask and command you in the name of King Solomon your lord that you protect me from all of natures whims. Be my protector. By this great seal shall it be so.

10   Sit in silence and just feel the power of God coursing through you. Visualize the power coming though the top of your head and out of your hands into the talisman. Watch it glow.

11   Place the Talisman down and say "May I be immune to the chaotic nature of mother earth and her tempests.

12   Leave the talisman on the Altar until the candle and incense are extinguished.

13   When the candles and Incense have burned down, you are free to use the talisman how you please; you can wear it,

put in your pocket or whatever is most appropriate for you based on the purpose of the talisman.

Ritual 41 – Talisman to Protect You From Poltergeists and Hauntings.
The Third Pentacle of the Moon

Ritual should be done On a Monday

1.   Setup the Altar as such: The Talisman will always be in the middle. On the right side, place the candle/s. On the left Place the Incense.

2.   Charge the Talisman

3   Light the Silver Candle

4   Light the incense

5   Pick up the talisman and place it your hands (Either hand or both)

6   Now sit in front of your altar and think about your situation. Are you being plagued by a haunting? Or entering a place that is haunted? Once you have built a sufficient feeling and image of what it is you want.

7   Now say the following verse with conviction: "Be pleased O God to deliver me, O God make haste to help me".

8   Now Invoke the angel/s:

Oh protector angel Aub I ask and command you in the name of King Solomon your lord that you protect me from all spirits that want to harm me or the ones I love. Be my protector. By this great seal shall it be so.

Oh Guardian Vevaphel I ask and command you in the name of King Solomon your lord that you banish all spirits that wish to harm me. By this great seal shall it be so.

9   Sit in silence and just feel the power of God coursing through you. Visualize the power coming though the top of your head and out of your hands into the talisman. Watch it glow.

10   Place the Talisman down and say "Oh great angels go forth in front of me and protect me from the evils that have come from the other side. So Mote it be.

11   Leave the talisman on the Altar until the candle and incense are extinguished.

12   When the candles and Incense have burned down, you are free to use the talisman how you please; you can wear it, put in your pocket or whatever is most appropriate for you based on the purpose of the talisman.

Ritual 42 – Talisman to Teach You the Properties of Crystals and Herbs

The Fourth Pentacle of the Moon

Ritual should be done On a Monday

1   Setup the Altar as such: The Talisman will always be in the middle. On the right side, place the candle/s. On the left Place the Incense.

2   Charge the Talisman

3   Light the Silver Candle

4   Light the incense

5   Pick up the talisman and place it your hands (Either hand or both)

6   Now sit in front of your altar and think about your desire to learn about the powers of Crystals and Herbs. Once you have built a sufficient feeling and image of what it is you want.

7   Now say the following verse with conviction: "Let them be confounded who persecute me, and let me not be confounded; let them fear, and not I" (It is not 100% clear why the verse doesn't seem consistent with the talismans purpose but we shall assume the manuscripts are correct.)

8   Now Invoke the name of God: Oh great God Eheieh Asher Eheieh that is the name you said unto Moses, your faithful servant. Teach unto me the secrets of the powers of nature. May the stones and plants whisper their secrets in my soul"

9   Now Invoke the angel/s:

Oh protector angel Yahel I ask and command you in the name of King Solomon your lord that you teach me the hidden wisdom found in the majesty of the stone and the herb. By this great seal shall it be so.

Oh Great teacher Sofiel I ask and command you in the name of King Solomon your lord that you teach me what I want to know regarding the wonderful works of nature and the properties therein. I command you by this great seal shall it be so.

10   Sit in silence and just feel the power of God coursing through you. Visualize the power coming though the top of your head and out of your hands into the talisman. Watch it glow.

11   Place the Talisman down and say "Oh great angels of Eheieh be though my teachers of nature as I requested. Amen

12   Leave the talisman on the Altar until the candle and incense are extinguished.

13   When the candles and Incense have burned down, you are free to use the talisman how you please; you can wear it, put in your pocket or whatever is most appropriate for you based on the purpose of the talisman.

Ritual 43 – Talisman to Achieve Precognitive Dreams
The Fifth Pentacle of the Moon

Ritual should be done On a Monday

1	Setup the Altar as such: The Talisman will always be in the middle. On the right side, place the candle/s. On the left Place the Incense.

2	Charge the Talisman

3	Light the Silver Candle

4	Light the incense

5   Pick up the talisman and place it your hands (Either hand or both)

6   Now sit in front of your altar and think about your desire to have precognitive dreams. Once you have built a sufficient feeling and image of what it is you want.

7   Now say the following verse with conviction: "Let God arise, and let His enemies be scattered; let them also who hate Him flee before Him." (It is not 100% clear why the verse doesn't seem consistent with the talismans purpose but we shall assume the manuscripts are correct.)

8   Now Invoke the name of God: Oh great God YHVH-ELOHIM that is the name you revealed yourself to Jacob who had visions in his sleep. I ask that I too will be the recipient of great visions in my sleep, but this seal so it shall be done.

9   Now Invoke the angel/s:

Oh protector angel Iachadiel I ask and command you in the name of King Solomon your lord that you protect me at night as I receive my vision in slumber. Protect me from spirits that lie. By this great seal shall it be so.

Oh Great teacher and Spirit guide Azarel I ask and command you in the name of King Solomon your lord that you teach me what I want to know in my sleep, give me visions. I command you by this great seal shall it be so.

10   Sit in silence and just feel the power of God coursing through you. Visualize the power coming though the top of your head and out of your hands into the talisman. Watch it glow.

11   Place the Talisman down and say "Oh great angels of YHVH-ELOHIM be though my teachers of as I sleep. Amen

12   Leave the talisman on the Altar until the candle and incense are extinguished.

13   When the candles and Incense have burned down, you are free to use the talisman how you please; you can wear it, put in your pocket or whatever is most appropriate for you based on the purpose of the talisman.

Ritual 44 – Talisman to Control the Weather
The Sixth Pentacle of the Moon

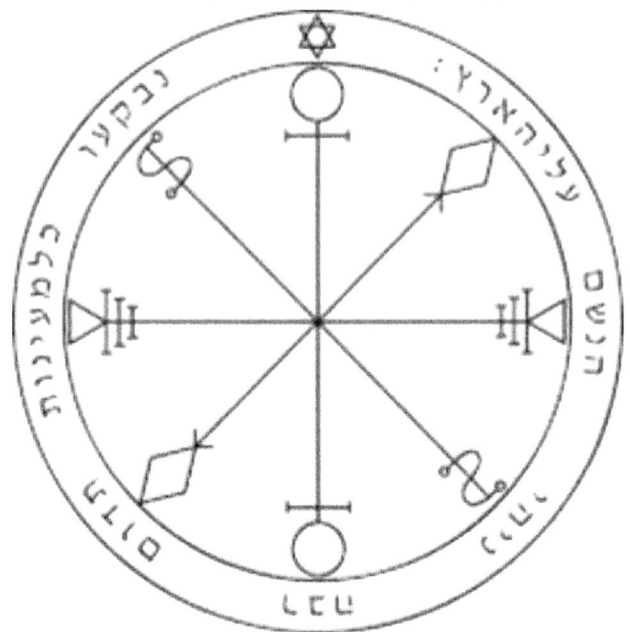

It is said that this Talisman can allow you to manipulate the weather as to cause heavy rains to come forth. Supposedly, if you keep this in water, the rain will continue until it is taken out.

Ritual should be done On a Monday

1. Setup the Altar as such: The Talisman will always be in the middle. On the right side, place the candle/s. On the left Place the Incense.

2. Charge the Talisman

3. Light the Silver Candle

4. Light the incense

5   Pick up the talisman and place it your hands (Either hand or both)

6   Now sit in front of your altar and think about your desire to control the weather with the power of the moon. Once you have built a sufficient feeling and image of what it is you want.

7   Now say the following verse with conviction: "All the fountains of the great deep were broken up... and the rain was upon the earth."

8   Sit in silence and just feel the power of God coursing through you. Visualize the power coming though the top of your head and out of your hands into the talisman. Watch it glow.

9   Place the Talisman down and say "By the great power of the Moon, I will control the weather as did the Great and Mighty King Solomon.

10   Leave the talisman on the Altar until the candle and incense are extinguished.

11   When the candles and Incense have burned down, you are free to use the talisman how you please; you can wear it, put in your pocket or whatever is most appropriate for you based on the purpose of the talisman.

There you have it, as you can see, these rituals are very easy. If you have read my other books, you will know that this is keeping to my magickal tradition. There is no reason to make magick so difficult. Many people have since attested that the paired down approach I teach has helped them not only with their own magick, but also their larger conception of who they are. In the next chapter I am just going to supply two images of Seals Ascribed to Solomon that are not as well known. I won't go into depth with them, save one that I think is important. Let us proceed.

Lesser-Known Seals of Solomon

In this chapter I will supply you with some illustration of a few lesser-known talismans. I will also supply two Islamic talisman that are also ascribed to Solomon. As you know, Solomon has a rich tradition in Islam.

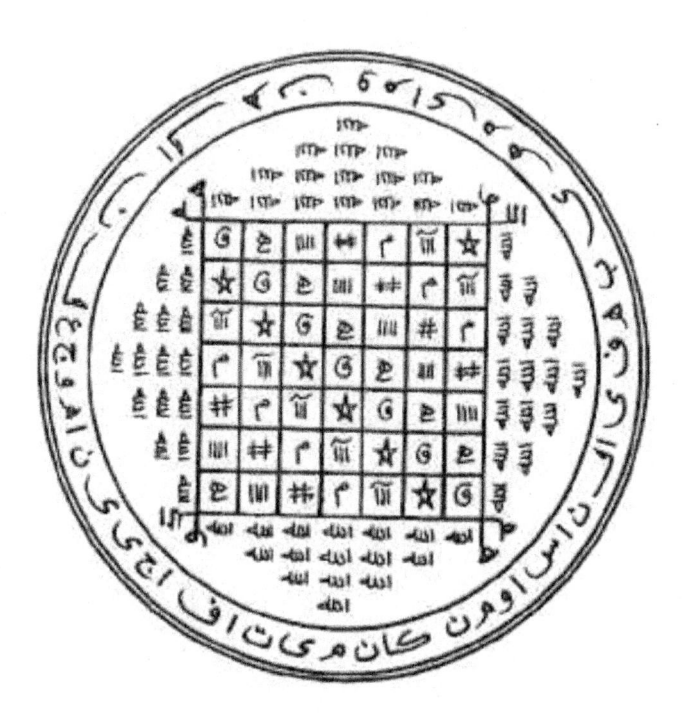

The above Talisman is ascribed to Solomon and is considered to be one that brings great success.

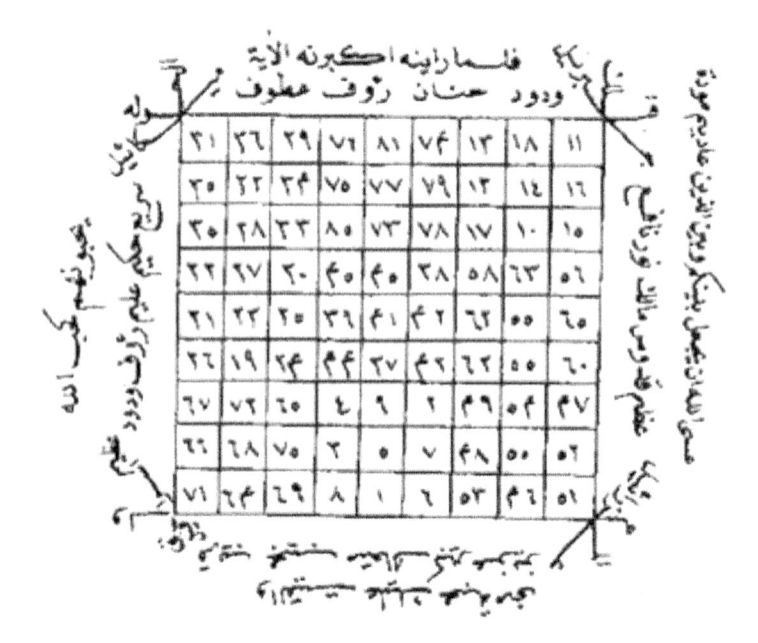

The above Talisman is ascribed to Solomon and is considered to be one that will help you attract anyone to you.

The Next Talisman is by far the most important in this tradition.

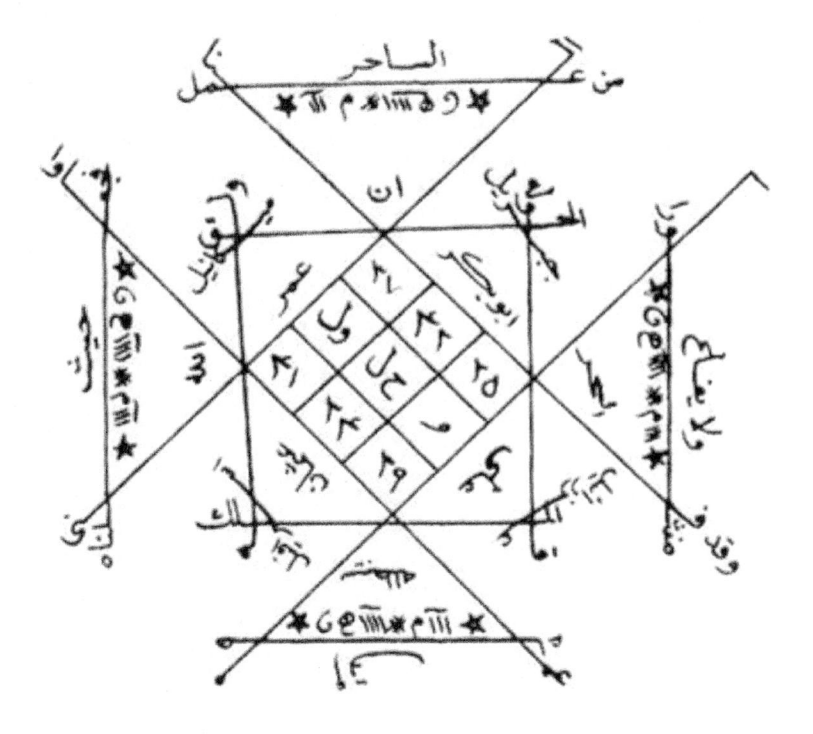

This one is in Arabic is called taweedat all azim (sp) or great talismans. This is an Islamic talisman of protection and can also cure diseases. It is said to contain 1000 angels or perhaps 1000 Jinn bound to it. Often in Islamic amulets, it is jinn that are bound and sometimes another entity type called Ilmu Khodam. This amulet is exceedingly rare, and you wont find many instances of this. The reason why you will not find this amulet as with other Islamic amulets ascribed to Solomon in general is because most grimoires have a decidedly Judeo-Christian bent as I mentioned earlier which that does not touch upon the rich Islamic Solomonic tradition of magick. The talisman, however, is constructed in similar fashion to many others with spiritual entities and names of God. (I see allah written several times here) and In the center is a numeric magickal square. It is a very powerful talisman.

I have not included rituals for these since I could not find the appropriate words. However, if you like, you may find ones comparable in the previous chapter and perhaps use those words. Let me know how it works for you.

Conclusion

We finally made it to the end my friend. I hope you were enriched by this book. It took me a long time to compile it since I had many notes from many years ago that I had to take out of old notebooks from my early days in the occult. I feel very strongly that once you use the Talismans in this book using my method you will never approach talismans the same way again. Many have attested to my paired down approach, and I am hoping you will find it useful as well. Until next time.

Occult Courses

Over the years, I have received many hundreds of emails asking me if I would ever consider creating online video courses. At first, I was unsure. After so many emails, I decided it was time.

I am now offering courses.

If it interests you in learning more about the **Occult, Meditation, Ancient Languages and History**, you will not be disappointed.

All courses will all be accessible, informative and affordable.

Please go to www.occultcourses.com

There you will find my current courses and all the upcoming courses. If you see a current course you are interested in, you can sign up and get **instant access.**

If you see a future course that interests you, sign up to the mailing list and I will notify you upon its release.

All courses come with a **30-day, no questions asked, money-back guarantee**. If a course is not for you, just let me know, and I will refund you.

Please go to www.occultcourses.com

Want to Enhance Your Rituals?

I am not one to promote myself. I like to keep things low-key, but I created a new service that has proven to enhance your rituals and your state of mind and I am very excited about it. As many of you may know, I use Brainwave Entrainment Audios to enhance my writing, my rituals and a lot more. I have been using brainwave products since the 80s. I am using one now as I write this.

I have created hyper-specific Brainwave audios geared to specific spiritual entities. For example, if you call upon the demon, King Paimon, I have a specific audio for him. If you work with the Hindus Goddess Lakshmi, I have a Brainwave Audio for her as well.

Please visit: **www.occultmindscapes.com**

I am adding Audios every week and will have something for everyone and for every tradition. I am only charging $3.95 per audio MP3 download, with steep discounts for multiple purchases.

I think you will LOVE them. My beta testers loved them and I am confident you will find them useful as well.

About Baal Kadmon

Baal Kadmon is an Author, and Occultist based out of New York City. In addition to the Occult, he is a Religious Scholar, Philosopher and a Historian specializing in Ancient History, Late Antiquity and Medieval History. He has studied and speaks Israeli Hebrew · Classical Hebrew · Ugaritic language · Arabic · Judeo-Aramaic · Syriac (language) · Ancient Greek and Classical Latin.

Baal first discovered his occult calling when he was very young. It was only in his teens, when on a trip to the Middle East that he heeded the call. Several teachers and many decades later he felt ready to share what he has learned.

His teachings are unconventional to say the least. He includes in-depth history in almost all the books he writes, in addition to rituals. He shatters the beloved and idolatrously held notions most occultists hold dear. His pared-down approach to magick is refreshing and is very much needed in a field that is mired by self-important magicians who place more importance on pomp and circumstance rather than on magick. What you learn from Baal is straight forward, with no frills. Magick is about bringing about change or a desired result; Magick is a natural birthright…There is no need to complicate it.

Follow Him On Facebook and other Social Media Sites:

http://baalkadmon.com/social-media/

Other Books By The Author

Organized by date of publication from most recent:

Surya Mantra Magick (Mantra Magick Series Book 13)

Tiamat Unveiled (Mesopotamian Magick Book 3)

Pazuzu Rising (Mesopotamian Magick Book 2)

BAAL: THE LORD OF THE HEAVENS: CALLING DOWN THE GREAT GOD OF CANAAN (CANAANITE MAGICK Book 2)

Chod Practice Demystified: Severing the Ties That Bind (Baal on Buddhism Book 2)

The Talmud: An Occultist Introduction

The Path of the Pendulum: An Unconventional Approach

Durga Mantra Magick: Harnessing The Power of the Divine Protectress

Asherah: The Queen of Heaven (Canaanite Magick Book 1)

Dependent Origination for the Layman (Baal on Buddhism Book 1)

The Watchers And Their Ways

Rabbi Isaac Luria: The Lion of the Kabbalah (Jewish Mystics Book 1)

Circe's Wand: Empowerment, Enchantment, Magick

Ganesha Mantra Magick: Calling Upon the God of New Beginnings

Shiva Mantra Magick: Harnessing The Primordial

Tefillin Magick: Using Tefillin For Magickal Purposes (Jewish Magick Book 1)

Jesus Magick (Bible Magick Book 2)

The Magickal Moment Of Now: The Inner Mind of the Advanced Magician

The Magick Of Lilith: Calling Upon The Great Goddess of The Left Hand Path (Mesopotamian Magick Book 1)

The Magickal Talismans of King Solomon

Mahavidya Mantra Magick: Tap Into the 10 Goddesses of Power

Jinn Magick: How to Bind the Jinn to do Your Bidding

Magick And The Bible: Is Magick Compatible With The Bible? (Bible Magick Book 1)

The Magickal Rites of Prosperity: Using Different Methods To Magickally Manifest Wealth

Lakshmi Mantra Magick: Tap Into The Goddess Lakshmi for Wealth and Abundance In All Areas of Life

Tarot Magick: Harness the Magickal Power of the Tarot

The Quantum Magician: Enhancing Your Magick With A Parallel Life

Tibetan Mantra Magick: Tap Into The Power Of Tibetan Mantras

The 42 Letter Name of God: The Mystical Name Of Manifestation (Sacred Names Book 6)

Tara Mantra Magick: How To Use The Power Of The Goddess Tara

Vedic Magick: Using Ancient Vedic Spells To Attain Wealth

The Daemonic Companion: Creating Daemonic Entities To Do Your Will

Tap Into The Power Of The Chant: Attaining Supernatural Abilities Using Mantras (Supernatural Attainments Series

72 Demons Of The Name: Calling Upon The Great Demons Of The Name (Sacred Names Book 5)

Moldavite Magick: Tap Into The Stone Of Transformation Using Mantras (Crystal Mantra Magick Book 1)

Ouija Board Magick - Archangels Edition: Communicate And Harness The Power Of The Great Archangels

Chakra Mantra Magick: Tap Into The Magick Of Your Chakras (Mantra Magick Series Book 4)

Seed Mantra Magick: Master The Primordial Sounds Of The Universe (Mantra Magick Series Book 3)

The Magick Of Saint Expedite: Tap Into The Truly Miraculous Power Of Saint Expedite (Magick Of The Saints Book 2)

Kali Mantra Magick: Summoning The Dark Powers of Kali Ma (Mantra Magick Series Book 2)

Mary Magick: Calling Forth The Divine Mother For Help (Magick Of The Saints Book 1)

Vashikaran Magick: Learn The Dark Mantras Of Subjugation (Mantra Magick Series Book 1)

The Hidden Names Of Genesis: Tap Into The Hidden Power Of Manifestation (Sacred Names Book 4)

The 99 Names Of Allah: Acquiring the 99 Divine Qualities of God (Sacred Names Book 3)

The 72 Angels Of The Name: Calling On the 72 Angels of God (Sacred Names)

The 72 Names of God: The 72 Keys To Transformation (Sacred Names Book 1)